BITTER SWEET

by Noël Coward

Copyright © 1929 by Noël Coward
Copyright © Words and Music 1929 by Chappell & Co Ltd
All Rights Reserved

BITTER SWEET is fully protected under the copyright laws of the British Commonwealth, including Canada, the United States of America, and all other countries of the Copyright Union. All rights, including professional and amateur stage productions, recitation, lecturing, public reading, motion picture, radio broadcasting, television and the rights of translation into foreign languages are strictly reserved.

ISBN 978-0-573-08005-0

www.concordtheatricals.co.uk

www.concordtheatricals.com

FOR AMATEUR PRODUCTION ENQUIRIES

UNITED KINGDOM AND WORLD EXCLUDING NORTH AMERICA

licensing@concordtheatricals.co.uk

020-7054-7200

Each title is subject to availability from Concord Theatricals, depending upon country of performance.

CAUTION: Professional and amateur producers are hereby warned that *BITTER SWEET* is subject to a licensing fee. Publication of this play does not imply availability for performance. Both amateurs and professionals considering a production are strongly advised to apply to the appropriate agent before starting rehearsals, advertising, or booking a theatre. A licensing fee must be paid whether the title is presented for charity or gain and whether or not admission is charged.

The Professional Rights in this play are controlled by Alan Brodie Representation, 55 Charterhouse St, Farringdon, London EC1M 6HA.

This work is published by Samuel French, an imprint of Concord Theatricals.

No one shall make any changes in this title for the purpose of production. No part of this book may be reproduced, stored in a retrieval system, or transmitted in any form, by any means, now known or yet to be invented, including mechanical, electronic, photocopying, recording, videotaping, or otherwise, without the prior written permission of the publisher. No one shall upload this title, or part of this title, to any social media websites.

The right of Noël Coward to be identified as author of this work has been asserted in accordance with Section 77 of the Copyright, Designs and Patents Act 1988.

MUSIC USE NOTE

Licensees are solely responsible for obtaining formal written permission from copyright owners to use copyrighted music in the performance of this play and are strongly cautioned to do so. If no such permission is obtained by the licensee, then the licensee must use only original music that the licensee owns and controls. Licensees are solely responsible and liable for all music clearances and shall indemnify the copyright owners of the play(s) and their licensing agent, Concord Theatricals, against any costs, expenses, losses and liabilities arising from the use of music by licensees. Please contact the appropriate music licensing authority in your territory for the rights to any incidental music.

IMPORTANT BILLING AND CREDIT REQUIREMENTS

If you have obtained performance rights to this title, please refer to your licensing agreement for important billing and credit requirements.

USE OF COPYRIGHT MUSIC

A licence issued by Concord Theatricals to perform this play does not include permission to use the incidental music specified in this copy. Where the place of performance is already licensed by the PERFORMING RIGHT SOCIETY (PRS) a return of the music used must be made to them. If the place of performance is not so licensed then application should be made to the PRS, 2 Pancras Square, London, N1C 4AG. A separate and additional licence from PHONOGRAPHIC PERFORMANCE LTD, 1 Upper James Street, London W1F 9DE (www.ppluk.com) is needed whenever commercial recordings are used.

BITTER SWEET

Originally produced at His Majesty's Theatre, London, on July 18th, 1929, with the following cast

THE MARCHIONESS OF SHAYNE (SARAH MILLICK)	Peggy Wood
CARL LINDEN	George Metaxa
MANON	Ivy St. Helier
DOLLY CHAMBERLAIN	Dorothy Boyd
LORD HENRY JEKYLL	William Harn
THE HON. HUGH DEVON	Robert Newton
MRS. MILLICK	Elaine Inescott
SIR ARTHUR FENCHURCH	Clifford Heatherley
HERR SCHLICK	Clifford Heatherley
LADY DEVON	Winifred Davis
THE MARQUIS OF STEERE	Robert Algar
VINCENT HOWARD	Billy Milton
LORD EDGAR JAMES	Victor Robson
LORD SORREL	Gerald Nodin
MR. VALE	Peter Gibson
MR. BETHEL	John Gatrell
MR. PROUTIE	Richard Cornish
VICTORIA	José Fearon
HARRIET	Maie Drage
GLORIA	Rose Hignell
HONOR	Eva Sternroyd
JANE	Eileen Carey
EFFIE	Mary Pounds
GUSSI	Norah Howard
LOTTE	Millie Sim
FREDA	Betty Huntley Wright
HANSI	Marjorie Rogers
LIEUTENANT TRANISCH	Arthur Alexander
CAPTAIN AUGUST LUTTE	Austin Trevor
MARQUIS OF SHAYNE	Alan Napier
NITA	Joan Panter
HELEN	Nancy Bevill
JACKIE	Maureen Moore

MRS. DEVON	Keira Tuson
VERNON CRAFT	Eric Lauriston
LORD HENRY JADE	Penryn Bannerman
CEDRIC BALLANTYNE	William Harn
BERTRAM SELLICK	Hugh Cuenod
PARKER	Claude Farrow
BURLEY	Anthony Brian
ACCOMPANIST	Leonard Pearce
SINGER	—
FRITZ	—

SIX PRATER GIRLS, FOUR FOOTMEN, THREE MUSICIANS, SIX WAITERS, FOUR CLEANERS, TWO CHARWOMEN, GUESTS AND CUSTOMERS

CHARACTERS

THE MARCHIONESS OF SHAYNE (SARAH MILLICK)
CARL LINDEN
MANON
DOLLY CHAMBERLAIN
LORD HENRY JEKYLL
THE HON. HUGH DEVON
MRS. MILLICK
SIR ARTHUR FENCHURCH
HERR SCHLICK
LADY DEVON
THE MARQUIS OF STEERE
VINCENT HOWARD
LORD EDGAR JAMES (Rifle Brigade Officer)
LORD SORREL (Artillery Officer)
MR. VALE (Naval Officer)
MR. BETHEL
MR. PROUTIE (Scotch Officer)
VICTORIA
HARRIET
GLORIA
HONOR
JANE
EFFIE
GUSSI
LOTTE
FREDA
HANSI
LIEUTENANT TRANISCH
CAPTAIN AUGUST LUTTE
MARQUIS OF SHAYNE
NITA
HELEN
JACKIE
MRS. DEVON
VERNON CRAFT
LORD HENRY JADE
CEDRIC BALLANTYNE
BERTRAM SELLICK
PARKER (Butler, ACT I, Scene One)
BURLEY (Butler, ACT III, Scene One)

ACCOMPANIST (ACT III, Scene One)
SINGER (ACT I, Scene One)
FRITZ
SIX PLATTER GIRLS
FOUR FOOTMEN
THREE MUSICIANS
SIX WAITERS
FOUR CLEANERS
TWO CHARWOMEN
GUESTS
CUSTOMERS

SYNOPSIS OF SCENES

ACT I

Scene One – Lady Shayne's House in Grosvenor Square. (Present Day.)
Scene Two – The Millicks' House in Belgrave Square. (1875)
Scene Three – The Ballroom of the Millicks' House. (1875)

ACT II

Scene One – Herr Schlick's Café in Vienna. (1880) Time:12 o'clock noon.
Scene Two – Herr Schlick's Café in Vienna. (1880) Time – 2 am.

ACT III

Scene One – Lord Shayne's House in Grosvenor Square. (1895.)
Scene Two – Same as ACT I, Scene One.

INDEX OF VOICES REQUIRED FOR SINGING PARTS

THE MARCHIONESS OF SHAYNE (SARAH MILLICK)	Soprano
CARL LINDEN	Tenor
MANON	Mezzo-Soprano
MARQUIS OF STEERE	Tenor
LORD EDGAR JAMES	Baritone
LORD SORREL	Bass
MR. VALE	Baritone
MR. BETHEL	Baritone
MR. PROUTIE	Top Tenor
VICTORIA	High Soprano
HARRIET	Mezzo
GLORIA	Soprano
HONOR	Deep Contralto
JANE	Contralto
EFFIE	Contralto
GUSSI	Mezzo
LOTTE	Mezzo
FREDA	Mezzo
HANSI	Mezzo
LIEUTENANT TRANISCH	Baritone
NITA	Mezzo
HELEN	Mezzo
JACKIE	Mezzo
SINGER (ACT I, Scene One)	Top Tenor
VERNON CRAFT	Baritone
LORD HENRY JADE	Baritone
CEDRIC BALLANTYNE	Baritone
BERTRAM SELLICK	Baritone

THE FOOTMEN should consist of	2 Basses and 2 Baritones	
THE CLEANERS " "	2 Sopranos and 2 Contraltos	
THE CHARWOMEN " "	1 Soprano "	1 Contralto
THE WAITERS " "	3 Tenors "	3 Basses

ACT I

Scene One

LADY SHANE's *house in Grosvenor Square at the present day.*

At right are two French windows leading to a balcony and by the windows is a jazz band consisting of **VINCENT HOWARD**, *the leader and pianist, a saxophone, a drummer and a singer. Up right centre are large double doors leading to a hall. Up left centre are similar doors leading to the supper room. Down left is a smaller door leading to the library. Small tables by the walls up centre and down left. Chairs at sides to dress the scene, leaving the centre clear for dancing. A settee is placed diagonally up left.*

Lighting: Pink, white and amber in floats and battens. Lengths, floods and spots as required. Fittings alight.

About ten couples are dancing a foxtrot.

At the music cue at the end of the overture the curtain rises and simultaneously the jazz band on stage takes up its cue to play **"THAT WONDERFUL MELODY"**.

When the curtain rises the stage is crowded with dancers (about ten couples), and the conversation and laughter combined with the band music should give an effect almost of pandemonium.

SINGER *(through his megaphone)*
   PLAY SOMETHING ROMANTIC,
   PLAY ME A ROMANTIC TUNE.
   I'M WEARY OF FRANTIC SYNCOPATION,
   JAZZ SENSATION PLAYED BY A CROON.
   PLAY ME SOMETHING ROMANTIC
   AS SWEET AS CAN BE.
   CARES WILL NOT DISMAY ME,
   IF YOU'LL JUST SIT DOWN AND PLAY ME
   A ROMANTIC MELODY.

The music comes to an end with the usual flourish and there is a smattering of applause from the dancers. **PARKER** *throws open the double doors up left centre and announces supper. All go in laughing and talking and can be seen taking their places at small tables. The double doors are closed by* **PARKER** *and the members of the band retire on to the balcony for a little fresh air, with the exception of* **VINCENT HOWARD,** *who remains at the piano improvising syncopations softly.*

DOLLY CHAMBERLAIN *and* **HENRY JEKYLL** *come in from the library.* **DOLLY** *is pretty and attractive, about twenty.* **HENRY** *is a trifle older and inclined to be faintly pompous.*

DOLLY *(going towards supper-room)* They've all gone in to supper—come on.

HENRY It's damned hot. *(Flings himself on to settee up left)*

DOLLY *(stopping and turning to him)* You've been grumbling about one thing and another all the evening.

HENRY Sorry, old darling.

DOLLY *(goes to settee and sits right of him)* Do you think you love me really?

HENRY Of course. Don't be an ass.

DOLLY Enough?

HENRY Enough for what?

DOLLY *(rises and crosses to centre)* Oh, I don't know—enough to spend your life with me, I suppose.

HENRY It's a little late to worry about that now—with the wedding next Monday.

> **VINCENT** *strikes a chord with some viciousness.* **DOLLY** *looks sharply over her shoulder at him. She crosses down left and takes a cigarette from the box on table.* **VINCENT** *goes on improvising.*

DOLLY You're right, it is hot.

HENRY Where's Lady Shayne?

DOLLY *(pointing to supper-room)* In there, I expect.

HENRY Strange old girl.

DOLLY I hope I shall be like that when I'm seventy. *(Lighting cigarette)*

HENRY She can't be as much as that.

DOLLY She is—she was at school with my grandmother.

HENRY Good God!

DOLLY It must be funny to look back over so many years. I wonder if she minds.

HENRY Minds what?

DOLLY Being old, of course *(looks at* **VINCENT***)* —to have led such a thrilling life and then suddenly to realize there's nothing left to look forward to.

HENRY *(rises and crosses to centre)* Well, she certainly is a gay old bird.

DOLLY *(going up to left of him)* Henry! *(She looks at him almost shocked)*

HENRY What?

DOLLY How silly that sounds—A gay old bird.

HENRY Well, it's true, isn't it? —That's what she is, always travelling around and giving parties and staying up all night—it's almost indecent—I wouldn't like to see my grandmother going on like that.

DOLLY Well, you needn't worry. *(She laughs)*

HENRY How do you mean?

DOLLY All your relations are too pompous to enjoy anything.

HENRY Dolly!

DOLLY Well, they are—they've all got several feet in the grave, there's no life left in them, if ever there was any, which I doubt—you'll probably be like that too in a few years.

HENRY You think Lady Shayne's life has been thrilling, do you? *(He smiles superciliously)* That's funny.

DOLLY Yes, I do—I do—and it isn't so funny either.

HENRY Now look here, Dolly, if you knew some of the things about Lady Shayne that *I* know—

DOLLY I know more than you know—I know that she justified her existence—she lived for something—

HENRY She was thoroughly immoral in her youth—lovers and awful second-rate people round her all the time. It was lucky for her she met Shayne and got back.

DOLLY Got back to what?

HENRY Decent people—society.

DOLLY Oh, dear. I can laugh now.

HENRY Now, Dolly, my girl—I—

He touches her. She recoils.

DOLLY *(suddenly with vehemence)* Shut up—shut up—go away from me—you're pompous and silly and I can't bear it—

HENRY Dolly!

DOLLY *(wildly)* Go away—go away!

HENRY You're impossible.

He stamps off into the supper-room.

As he opens the door the **GUESTS** *should be seen and heard enjoying themselves. As he shuts the door* **DOLLY** *crosses to settee up left and sits down miserably.*

VINCENT Can I stop playing now?

DOLLY *(in a stifled voice)* No—go on.

VINCENT I can't bear it much longer—darling.

DOLLY Vincent—don't.

VINCENT Please come over here and sit close to me.

DOLLY I'd better not, I think.

VINCENT Afraid?

DOLLY Yes.

She goes over and sits beside him, facing down stage—he goes on playing.

VINCENT I love you so. *(He stops improvising, kisses her and starts playing again)*

DOLLY Oh, God! I'm so utterly, utterly miserable. *(She buries her head in her arms)*

VINCENT *(stops playing)* Don't cry—you're going to marry a rich man and have rich friends and a rich house and rich food and some day if you're really rich enough you'll be able to engage me to come and play for you. *(He laughs bitterly)*

DOLLY How can you be so horrid!

VINCENT You'll be safe anyhow.

DOLLY I don't want to be safe.

VINCENT Come away with me then—I've got no money—nothing to offer you—you'd look fine singing my songs in some cheap cabaret somewhere—and living in third-rate hotels and just—well, earning your living—

DOLLY It sounds marvellous.

VINCENT Don't be a damned fool!

DOLLY Vincent—

VINCENT It's hell— (*He strikes some notes by running his finger across the keys, then rises and goes to the lower window right as though to go out*)

DOLLY Where are you going?

VINCENT (*stopping and turning to her*) To call the boys—we've got to work some more.

DOLLY I shan't see you again until—until—after I'm married.

VINCENT Never mind—safety first.

DOLLY What am I to do? — (*Rises and goes to right centre*) Oh, what am I to do?

VINCENT (*crosses to right of her*) Goodbye, you poor little kid—

He suddenly takes her in his arms and kisses her. She twines her arms round his neck and they stand there clasped tight. **LADY SHAYNE** *enters from the supper-room. (The* **GUESTS** *are seen and heard as the door opens) She watches them silently for a moment. She is seventy years old, but her figure is still slim; her hair is snow white, and her gown is exquisite. She has a walking stick.*

LADY SHAYNE (*as she reaches centre*) Dolly!

DOLLY *and* **VINCENT** *break away from each other.*

I come on an errand of peace from your fiancé. If it is inopportune, I apologize.

DOLLY Oh, Lady Shayne.

LADY SHAYNE *(to* **VINCENT***)* You are the piano player in the band, aren't you?

VINCENT I'm the leader of the band.

LADY SHAYNE What a pity! It's not a very good band.

VINCENT I'm sorry for what happened just now, your ladyship. It—it was an accident.

LADY SHAYNE In what way—an accident?

VINCENT I—er—we were saying goodbye.

LADY SHAYNE Your drummer is too loud, and I can't bear the man who plays the saxophone.

DOLLY Lady Shayne—I—let me explain.

LADY SHAYNE When a man plays off key the only explanation is that he is a bad musician.

DOLLY Lady Shayne—I love Vincent and—and he loves me.

LADY SHAYNE And this is Vincent?

DOLLY Yes, of course.

LADY SHAYNE And you are sure he loves you? Would he live for you? Die for you?

VINCENT Oh! Come, your ladyship, is that necessary?

LADY SHAYNE Yes! Absolutely.

VINCENT Oh! (**LADY SHAYNE** *laughs*) You're laughing at us, your ladyship.

LADY SHAYNE I laugh at almost everything now—it's only when one is very old indeed that one can see the joke all the way round.

DOLLY What joke?

LADY SHAYNE Life and death and happiness and despair and love. *(She laughs again)*

VINCENT Don't laugh like that, please—your ladyship.

LADY SHAYNE So you're a musician—an amiable, sensitive-looking young man—and you've been making love to this child—or has she been making love to you? —everything seems to have changed round lately.

VINCENT It just happened—we—at least that is—I don't know.

LADY SHAYNE Are you a married man?

VINCENT No—of course not.

LADY SHAYNE Well, you needn't be so vehement. I merely thought you might have forgotten—

DOLLY Are you angry?

LADY SHAYNE Not in the least, my dear. What do you intend to do?

DOLLY I don't know.

LADY SHAYNE Well, if I were you I should make up my mind. (*She turns towards the supper-room*)

DOLLY You *are* angry.

LADY SHAYNE I detest indecision.

DOLLY I don't understand—

Several people come out of the supper-room, including **NITA** *and* **HELEN**, *who come down to left centre.*

NITA Dolly—what have you been doing to Henry—he's plunged in gloom.

HELEN He's sending out thought waves of depression and I got the lot, being next to him.

JACKIE *rushes out of the supper-room with several others. She goes to the piano.*

JACKIE What's happened to the band? Oh, Mr. Howard, play something—play something romantic—I want to dance.

LADY SHAYNE (*laughing*) Yes—play something romantic.

VINCENT *(savagely)* I'll play anything anybody wants—that's what I'm hired for— *(He goes to the piano)* Here's romance for you—how's this—

He plays a few bars of a swift jazz tune. Everyone begins to dance and jig about, **NITA** *Charlestons a few steps, while* **HELEN** *and* **JACKIE** *clap their hands and sing. Suddenly* **LADY SHAYNE** *taps the floor with her stick. All stop and look at her.* **JACKIE** *is on her left.* **DOLLY***, who has not danced, has remained close to her right.*

LADY SHAYNE Stop—stop—it's hideous—none of you know anything or want anything beyond noise and speed.

DOLLY What do you mean? What do you mean?

LADY SHAYNE Your dreams of romance are nightmares. Your conception of life grotesque. Come with me a little—I'll show you—listen—listen—

HELEN *(softly)* Oh God, what's the old girl up to now?

DOLLY Be quiet.

LADY SHAYNE *begins to sing—everyone squats down on the floor, some of them giggling furtively,* **VINCENT** *and* **DOLLY** *stare at her as though transfixed.*

"THE CALL OF LIFE"

LADY SHAYNE
>YOUR ROMANCE COULD NOT LIVE THE LENGTH OF A DAY,
>YOU HESITATE AND ANALYSE,
>BETRAY YOUR LOVE WITH COMPROMISE,
>TILL GLAMOUR FADES AWAY;
>AND ALL TOO SOON YOU REALIZE
>THAT THERE IS NOTHING LEFT TO SAY.

CHORUS
>HEY, HEY—HEY, HEY,
>HOW DOES SHE GET THAT WAY;
>SHE'D BE MORE LIGHT-HEARTED

IF SHE STARTED—TO CHARLESTON;
SHE'S NEVER DANCED IT,
SHE'S NEVER CHANCED IT;

MEN

PERHAPS HER MUSCLES ARE DISINCLINED,

CHORUS

PERHAPS SHE HASN'T THE STRENGTH OF MIND.

LADY SHAYNE

LOVE THAT'S TRUE CAN MEAN NAUGHT TO YOU BUT A NAME,
A THING THAT ISN'T PART OF YOU;
CAN NEVER TOUCH THE HEART OF YOU;
IT'S NOTHING BUT A GAME,
A FIRE WITHOUT A FLAME.

MEN

WE FIND IT DIFFICULT TO GRASP YOUR MEANING.

LADY SHAYNE Maybe the past is intervening.

The **CHORUS** *rises and groups round her in a semicircle.*

MEN

WE VERY MUCH REGRET THAT TIMES HAVE CHANGED SO,
LIFE IS MORE SPEEDILY ARRANGED SO.

All turn outwards and move away a little.

LADY SHAYNE

IN YOUR WORLD OF SWIFTLY TURNING WHEELS
LIFE MUST BE EXTREMELY GREY.

All turn towards her and stand round her again.

MEN

WE'VE NO TIME TO WASTE ON LOVE IDEALS,
THAT WHICH TO OUR SENSES MOST APPEALS
IS ALL WE CAN OBEY.

LADY SHAYNE

NO—NO. NOT SO;
THERE MUST BE SOMETHING FURTHER ON,

A VISION YOU CAN COUNT UPON,
TO HELP YOU TO ACQUIRE
A MEMORY WHEN YOUTH IS GONE
OF WHAT WAS ONCE YOUR HEART'S DESIRE.

All re-group, sitting round her as before. **DOLLY** *remains standing at right of her.*

THERE IS A CALL THAT ECHOES SWEETLY
WHEN IT IS SPRING AND LOVE IS IN THE AIR;
WHATE'ER BEFALL, RESPOND TO IT COMPLETELY,
THO' IT MAY BRING YOU SADNESS AND DESPAIR;
FLING FAR BEHIND YOU
THE CHAINS THAT BIND YOU,
THAT LOVE MAY FIND YOU
IN JOY OR STRIFE;
THO' FATE MAY CHEAT YOU,
AND DEFEAT YOU,
YOUR YOUTH MUST ANSWER TO THE CALL OF LIFE.

CHORUS

AH! —

Lighting – Gradually check out everything, the last to go being a front of house white spot on **LADY SHAYNE**, *which dies out on last word of song.*

LADY SHAYNE

THO' FATE MAY CHEAT YOU
AND DEFEAT YOU
YOUR YOUTH MUST ANSWER TO THE CALL OF LIFE.

The curtain is lowered immediately on the word "life".

Lighting – Working light on stage.

The change which follows must be done as quickly as possible. A quick change room on stage must be provided for **SARAH**. *The music continues throughout, and when ready,* **SARAH**'s *voice, now grown young, is heard singing in the darkness.*

SARAH

THO' FATE MAY CHEAT YOU
AND DEFEAT YOU,
YOUR YOUTH MUST ANSWER TO THE CALL OF LIFE.

On the last note the curtain is raised.

Lighting – Before the curtain is raised the working light should be blacked out.

Then, as the curtain rises, fade in slowly floats white and amber to 3/4. Lengths, spots and floods as required. Fittings out.

Scene Two

The music-room of the **MILLICKS'** *house in Belgrave Square in 1875.*

There are two large windows at the back with a sofa in front of them. A grand piano is at left with the keys to right. The only door is right.

SARAH *is standing centre facing front,* **CARL** *is seated at the piano and strikes the last chord with the orchestra as it finishes.*

When **SARAH** *finishes singing,* **CARL** *allows his hands to drop from the keys, and still gazing into her eyes, he speaks:*

CARL That was excellent, Miss Sarah—you are improving in a very marked manner.

SARAH *(demurely)* Thank you.

CARL *(rises and moves towards her a little)* I wrote that song for you when I was sixteen years old.

SARAH But, Mr Linden, that cannot be true—we have only known each other during the past year.

CARL I mean that I wrote it for someone like you.

SARAH *(quickly)* Oh!

CARL Not a real person—just an ideal in my mind, someone young and charming—holding out her arms as you did just now—expectantly.

SARAH Expectant of what, Mr Linden?

CARL *(hopelessly turning away)* I don't know.

SARAH I think it is the loveliest song I ever heard.

CARL *(looking at her again)* Do you?

SARAH *(meeting his eyes)* Yes—of course.

CARL You took the high note too much at the back of your throat.

SARAH *(sits on sofa)* I'm sorry.

CARL It doesn't matter.

SARAH Oh, but, surely it does.

CARL Nothing matters but just these few moments. *(Goes to left end of sofa)*

SARAH Why do you say that, Mr Linden?

CARL Because it's spring, and I—I—

SARAH Yes?

CARL I fear I am talking nonsense.

SARAH *(smiling)* Perhaps a little.

CARL We have festivals in the spring in my country—and the young boys and girls dance and their clothes are brightly coloured, glinting in the sun, and the old people sit round under the trees, watching and tapping their sticks on the ground and reviving in their hearts memories of when they, too, were young and in love.

SARAH In love.

CARL Yes—as you are in love with your handsome Mr Devon.

SARAH Oh—Hugh—yes, of course. Tell me more about your country, Mr Linden.

CARL *(crosses to left below piano)* There is nothing to tell really—it seems so very far away—I've almost forgotten.

SARAH You're homesick though, I can see you are.

CARL Can you?

SARAH Perhaps it's the climate here, it *is* depressing—

CARL Yes, a little. *(He leans on the piano and sings, looking at her)*

THO' THERE MAY BE BEAUTY IN THIS LAND OF YOURS,
SKIES ARE VERY OFTEN DULL AND GREY;
IF I COULD BUT TAKE THAT LITTLE HAND OF YOURS,
JUST TO LEAD YOU SECRETLY AWAY,
WE WOULD WATCH THE DANUBE AS IT GENTLY FLOWS,
LIKE A SILVER RIBBON WINDING FREE;
EVEN AS I SPEAK OF IT MY LONGING GROWS,
ONCE AGAIN MY OWN DEAR LAND TO SEE.
IF YOU COULD ONLY COME WITH ME,
IF YOU COULD ONLY COME WITH ME.

SARAH (*staring straight in front of her*) Oh, Mr Linden.

CARL Yes.

SARAH How very strange everything is today.

CARL Will you forgive me, Miss Sarah, when I tell you that I shall be unable to play at your wedding reception.

SARAH (*disappointed*) Oh!

CARL I must go away on that day—to Brussels.

SARAH Brussels?

CARL (*hurriedly*) Yes, a concert—I have to play at a concert—it is very important.

SARAH I understand.

CARL Do you?

SARAH Yes—but it is very, very disappointing.

CARL But I am deeply grateful for the honour you have done me in asking me.

SARAH (*lightly, rising and moving right a little*) This is the last time we shall meet then for ever so long.

CARL Tonight—I am playing tonight for the dance.

SARAH But that is different. There will be so many people—

CARL (*crosses to centre*) This is indeed the last time we shall be alone together.

SARAH *(looking down)* Yes. *(Turns to him at centre)*

CARL You have been a charming pupil—I shall always look back on these months with happiness.

SARAH Happiness?

CARL And sadness too.

SARAH Oh, dear.

CARL There are tears in your eyes.

SARAH In yours also.

CARL I know—I am sorry to be so foolish.

SARAH Dear Mr Linden—

She gives him her hand, he kisses it fervently, then pulls himself together with a tremendous effort.

CARL Once more now—your exercises—just once more through. *(He goes to piano and sits)*

SARAH *(tearfully)* Very well.

CARL *strikes a chord.*

"I'LL SEE YOU AGAIN"

CARL
    NOW MISS SARAH, IF YOU PLEASE,
    SING A SCALE FOR ME.

SARAH
    AH—AH—AH—

CARL *(striking another chord)*
    TAKE A BREATH AND THEN REPRISE
    IN A DIFFERENT KEY.

SARAH
    AH—AH—AH—

CARL
    ALL MY LIFE I SHALL
        REMEMBER KNOWING
        YOU,
    ALL THE PLEASURE I HAVE
        FOUND IN SHOWING YOU
    THE DIFFERENT WAYS   **SARAH**
    THAT ONE MAY PHRASE   AH—AH—AH!
    THE CHANGING LIGHT, AND
        CHANGING SHADE;
    HAPPINESS THAT MUST DIE,
    MELODIES THAT MUST FLY,
    MEMORIES THAT MUST
        FADE,
    DUSTY AND FORGOTTEN BY
        AND BY.   **SARAH**
                                AH—AH—AH!

He rises and goes to left of her at centre.

SARAH
    LEARNING SCALES WILL
        NEVER SEEM SO SWEET
        AGAIN
    TILL OUR DESTINY SHALL
        LET US MEET AGAIN.

CARL   **SARAH**
    THE WILL OF FATE   AH—AH—AH!
    MAY COME TOO LATE.

SARAH
    WHEN I'M RECALLING THESE
        HOURS WE'VE HAD
    WHY WILL THE FOOLISH
        TEARS
    TREMBLE ACROSS THE
        YEARS,
    WHY SHALL I FEEL SO SAD,

CARL   **SARAH**
    TREASURING THE MEMORY   AH—AH—AH!
        OF THESE DAYS
        ALWAYS?

BOTH
    I'LL SEE YOU AGAIN,
    WHENEVER SPRING BREAKS
        THROUGH AGAIN;
    TIME MAY LIE HEAVY
        BETWEEN,
    BUT WHAT HAS BEEN
    IS PAST FORGETTING.
    THIS SWEET MEMORY,
    ACROSS THE YEARS WILL
        COME TO ME;
    THO' MY WORLD MAY GO
        AWRY,
    IN MY HEART WILL EVER LIE
    JUST THE ECHO OF A SIGH,
    GOODBYE.
    I'LL SEE YOU AGAIN,
    WHENEVER SPRING BREAKS
        THROUGH AGAIN;
    TIME MAY LIE HEAVY
        BETWEEN,
    BUT WHAT HAS BEEN
    IS PAST FORGETTING.
    SARAH *crosses left to right end of piano,* **CARL** *moves centre.*
    THIS SWEET MEMORY
    ACROSS THE YEARS WILL
        COME TO ME;
    THO' MY WORLD MAY GO
        AWRY,
    IN MY HEART WILL EVER LIE
    JUST THE ECHO OF A SIGH,
    GOODBYE.

    CARL *moves left to* **SARAH** *and kisses her hand. Voices off right are heard. They straighten out as* **MRS MILLICK** *enters and comes to right centre. She is followed by* **HUGH DEVON,** *who stands in the doorway. They both stand*

ACT I, SCENE TWO

still for a moment as though they suspected something and then **MRS MILLICK** *speaks.* **HUGH** *comes down stage right.* **CARL** *backs up stage centre a little, leaving the line clear between* **SARAH** *and her mother.*

MRS MILLICK Darling child—your lesson should have been over a quarter of an hour ago. There is so much to be done—I declare I'm nearly frantic—Hugh has been telling me about his aunt—poor Lady Ettleworth, she developed acute gastritis yesterday evening, and it may mean postponing the wedding, and on the other hand it may not. I'm certain it was the peas she ate at lunch here. They were like bullets. Good afternoon, Mr Linden.

CARL *(bowing)* Good afternoon, Mrs Millick.

HUGH Good afternoon.

CARL *(bowing)* Good afternoon.

HUGH You look tired, Sarah.

SARAH I am a little—I—it is quite hot today.

MRS. MILLICK I fear I must hurry you away, Mr. Linden—Sarah has a dressmaker at four-thirty—and there is so much to be done.

CARL I quite understand.

MRS. MILLICK Doubtless Sarah will resume her lessons with you when she is settled down in her new home.

SARAH Mother—I—please—

MRS MILLICK It will be an occupation. I always believe in young married women having an occupation.

CARL I should have thought being married would be sufficient.

MRS MILLICK *(slightly scandalized)* Mr Linden—

CARL *(bitterly)* Your daughter must learn from someone else when she is a young married woman, Mrs Millick. I shall not be here.

MRS MILLICK Well, I'm sure I'm very sorry, I—

CARL *(looking fixedly at* **SARAH***)* I shall be far away in my own country—but each year when spring comes round again, I shall remember you, Miss Sarah, and what a charming pupil you were, and how, although you sometimes sang your top notes from the back of your throat, and your middle notes through your nose, you always sang your deep notes from your heart. *(He bows to* **SARAH***)*

MRS MILLICK My dear Mr Linden!

CARL This is goodbye, Miss Sarah, except for tonight, when there will be so many people—too many people.

He bows abruptly to **MRS MILLICK** *and goes quickly out right, passing between* **MRS MILLICK** *and* **HUGH**. **HUGH** *advances towards* **SARAH**, *who goes up centre and falls sobbing on the sofa.* **MRS. MILLICK** *is going up to her as the curtain is lowered.*

Lighting – Front of house arcs and floats out.

Scene Three

The ballroom of the **MILLICKS'** *house in Belgrave Square in 1875, late in the evening.*

The ball is nearly over. There is a rostrum stretching right across the back of the set, except for a flight of stairs up right. At the back of the rostrum are three French windows looking out on to a balcony, beyond which is a view of the trees in the Square. At the left end of the rostrum is a small dance band consisting of **CARL** *the leader and first violin, a grand piano and another violinist. There are exits down right and left, up right and left and also at right and left ends of the balcony. There is also an exit up the stairs.*

Lighting – Full up everything. Fittings alight.

The music in the orchestra changes to a polka and when this has been played once through, the curtain rises, the stage band having joined in. There are about a dozen couples dancing an old-fashioned polka and enjoying it thoroughly. The six "bridesmaids", **VICTORIA, EFFIE, GLORIA, HONOR, HARRIET** *and* **JANE,** *and their partners* **LORD STEERE, MR BETHEL, MR PROUTIE, LORD SORREL, LORD EDGAR JAMES** *and* **MR VALE** *respectively, are dancing with the others. Several chaperones are seated round the sides and back. The polka continues until the music has been played through once more, then the men bow and the girls curtsey, the chaperones rise and all drift off by the balcony, stairs and other exits. The two bandsmen exit up left.* **CARL** *remains behind sorting music,* **LADY DEVON,** *who has been sitting on the settee at left of the stairs, rises, comes forward and meets* **MRS MILLICK** *at centre as she billows in from down left.*

LADY DEVON Charming, Violet—quite delightful—I congratulate you.

MRS MILLICK The young people seem very happy, I think.

LADY DEVON I thought Sarah looked radiant but a trifle flushed when she was waltzing with Hugh a little while ago.

MRS. MILLICK She has been flushed all the evening. I hope she isn't feverish—I feel quite disturbed about her.

LADY DEVON I feel sure you have no cause to be—she was positively hilarious in the supper-room.

MRS MILLICK Unnaturally so.

LADY DEVON She is in love, my dear.

> **HUGH** *enters from the supper-room down left.*

HUGH *(in harassed tones as he goes to left of* **LADY DEVON***)* Oh, there you are.

LADY DEVON *(fondly)* Happy boy.

HUGH I am very worried.

MRS MILLICK Why—what has happened?

HUGH Sarah is behaving in a most peculiar manner—she spilt a full glass of claret cup over Sir Arthur Fenchurch and laughed.

MRS MILLICK Laughed!

LADY DEVON Sir Arthur—Good heavens!

> **SIR ARTHUR** *enters from down left, he is a pompous-looking old gentleman. He is obviously restraining a boiling fury with a great effort. His shirt-front is claret-stained and his manner frigid. He comes to left centre, where he stands mopping his shirt-front with his handkerchief.*

SIR ARTHUR *(bowing to* **MRS MILLICK** *furiously, but politely)* A delightful evening, Mrs Millick—thank you a thousand times.

MRS MILLICK But, Sir Arthur—you mustn't think of going.

SIR ARTHUR I couldn't think of staying—so many fresh young people enjoying themselves so very thoroughly—I feel out of place.

LADY DEVON But, Sir Arthur—

SIR ARTHUR (*firmly as he crosses right in front of them*) Goodnight, Lady Devon. Goodnight, Mrs Millick. (*As he reaches the foot of the stairs he stops and turns to* **HUGH**) My boy—I sincerely *hope* your marriage will be a happy one.

He exits up right.

MRS MILLICK Well!

HUGH There now.

LADY DEVON How very, very unfortunate.

SARAH enters from down left and comes to left centre; she looks lovely, but her manner is strained and almost defiant.

SARAH Has he gone?

MRS MILLICK Sarah—I'm ashamed of you.

SARAH He patted my hand, mamma, then he patted my head. I detest being patted.

HUGH He's one of the most influential men in London.

MRS MILLICK And so kind.

SARAH And so pompous.

LADY DEVON Sarah!

MRS MILLICK The first thing tomorrow morning you shall write him a letter of apology.

She moves away with **LADY DEVON** *and both go out down left.* **SARAH** *moves to right centre.*

SARAH Tomorrow is so far away. (*She laughs*)

HUGH *(going to left of her)* I don't understand you tonight, Sarah.

SARAH I don't think I quite understand myself.

HUGH Why did you cry this afternoon in the music room?

SARAH Are you glad you are going to marry me, Hugh?

HUGH Why did you cry like that?

SARAH And will you be kind to me—always?

HUGH You haven't answered me.

SARAH And do you love me?

HUGH *(irritably)* Sarah!

SARAH Do you?

HUGH Of course I do—what is the matter with you?

> CARL LINDEN *stands up on the orchestra dais and very softly plays on the violin* **"I'LL SEE YOU AGAIN"**. SARAH *starts and then begins to laugh hysterically.*

SARAH Don't look so solemn, Hugh—I'm in love.

HUGH My dear girl, that's all very well—

SARAH Is it?

HUGH But you really must restrain yourself.

SARAH *(almost rudely, moving over to left centre)* What a stupid tune, Mr Linden—so dismal—

HUGH *(following her)* Sarah!

SARAH *(peremptorily)* Play something gay, please—immediately.

> CARL *stops playing.*

HUGH *(softly)* Sarah, you must not speak like that—have you taken leave of your senses?

SARAH *(vehemently)* Let me alone—please go away—let me alone!

ACT I, SCENE THREE

HUGH *goes out angrily down left.*

SARAH *stands at centre and starts to sing. The two bandsmen enter unobtrusively from up left and the stage band starts to follow the orchestra.*

"WHAT IS LOVE?"

SARAH *and* **CHORUS**.

SARAH
> PLAY SOMETHING GAY FOR ME,
> PLAY FOR ME, PLAY FOR ME;
> SET ME FREE,
> I AM IN A TRANCE TONIGHT,
> CAN'T YOU SEE
> HOW I WANT TO DANCE TONIGHT?
> MADLY MY HEART IS BEATING,
> SOME INSANE MELODY POSSESSING ME,
> IN MY BRAIN THRILLING AND OBSESSING ME;
> HOW CAN I LEAVE IT TO CALL IN VAIN?
> IS IT JOY OR PAIN?
> LIVE YOUR LIFE, FOR TIME IS FLEETING,
> SOME INSISTENT VOICE REPEATING;
> HEAR ME—HEAR ME,
> HOW CAN I LEAVE IT TO CALL IN VAIN?
> IS IT JOY OR PAIN?

Refrain.
> TELL ME—TELL ME—TELL ME, WHAT IS LOVE?
> IS IT SOME CONSUMING FLAME;
> PART OF THE MOON, PART OF THE SUN,
> PART OF A DREAM BARELY BEGUN?
> WHEN IS THE MOMENT OF BREAKING-WAKING?
> SKIES CHANGE, NOTHING IS THE SAME,
> SOME STRANGE MAGIC IS TO BLAME;
> VOICES, THAT SEEM TO ECHO ROUND ME AND ABOVE,
> TELL ME, WHAT IS LOVE, LOVE, LOVE?

The **CHORUS** *re-enter right and left and group in a circle round* **SARAH**, *who picks up her train and waltzes slowly round the stage by herself.*

CHORUS
SKIES CHANGE, NOTHING IS THE SAME,
SOME STRANGE MAGIC IS TO BLAME;

SARAH *(stopping at centre)*
VOICES THAT SEEM TO ECHO ROUND ME AND ABOVE,
TELL ME, WHAT IS LOVE, LOVE, LOVE?

SARAH
PLAY SOMETHING GAY FOR ME,
PLAY FOR ME—PLAY FOR ME;
TELL ME WHY
SPRING HAS SO ENCHANTED ME,
WHY THIS SHY
PASSION HAS BEEN GRANTED ME;
AM I AWAKE OR DREAMING?
FAR AND NEAR
EVERY LOVER FOLLOWS YOU,
SWIFT AND CLEAR,
FLYING AS THE SWALLOWS DO;
LEAVE ME NO LONGER TO CALL IN VAIN,
ARE YOU JOY OR PAIN?
LEAVE ME NOT BY LOVE FORSAKEN,
IF I SLEEP, THEN LET ME WAKEN;
HEAR ME—HEAR ME,
LEAVE ME NO LONGER TO CALL IN VAIN,
ARE YOU JOY OR PAIN?

CHORUS
TELL ME, TELL ME WHAT IS LOVE?
IS IT SOME CONSUMING FLAME;
PART OF THE MOON, PART OF THE SUN,
PART OF A DREAM BARELY BEGUN?

SARAH ⎫ WHEN IS THE MOMENT OF BREAKING-WAKING?
CHORUS ⎭ SKIES CHANGE, NOTHING IS THE SAME,
  SOME STRANGE MAGIC IS TO BLAME;

SARAH

VOICES, THAT SEEM TO ECHO IN THE AIR
ROUND ME AND ABOVE,
TELL ME, WHAT IS LOVE? AH! —

CHORUS

VOICES SEEM TO ECHO ROUND HER,
ECHO ROUND HER AND ABOVE HER.

SARAH ⎫ LEAVE ME NO LONGER TO CALL IN VAIN.
CHORUS ⎭

SARAH

TELL ME, WHAT IS LOVE,

SARAH ⎫ LOVE, LOVE?
CHORUS ⎭

The stage band then goes straight into **"GOD! SAVE THE QUEEN"**. *The full company stand to attention facing upstage while it is being played and then the party breaks up.* **MRS MILLICK** *enters up right and stands with* **SARAH** *at left of the arch leading to the stairs. They say goodnight to the guests, who exit up right.* **CARL** *crosses right, bows to* **MRS MILLICK** *and* **SARAH** *and exits up right. The other two bandsmen go out up left.* **HUGH** *comes in from the balcony left and meets* **SARAH**, *who has left her mother and wandered centre. Two guests are left talking to* **MRS MILLICK** *up right.*

SARAH I'm sorry, Hugh.

HUGH *(stiffly)* It doesn't matter.

SARAH Oh, but it does—I was unkind and silly.

HUGH It doesn't matter.

SARAH Will you please forgive me?

HUGH There is nothing to forgive.

SARAH I shall be bad again if you are so polite.

HUGH My dear Sarah!

SARAH *(desperately)* Are you always going to be like this—after we are married, I mean—cold and unbending?

HUGH I can only hope you are not often going to behave as you have tonight.

SARAH Oh, dear.

HUGH I don't feel that you realise yet the dignity of the position you will hold as my wife.

SARAH I am not your wife yet.

HUGH I enjoy being high-spirited as much as anyone.

SARAH Do you?

HUGH But there is a time and place for everything.

SARAH Then I can look forward to us being very high-spirited when we are alone—when no one is looking—you might wear a funny hat at breakfast.

HUGH I am very fond of you, my dear, but you must remember I am older than you.

SARAH Not so very much.

> **LADY DEVON** *enters from down right and joins* **MRS MILLICK** *by the stairs. The two guests have just left up right.*

HUGH And it is part of my profession to consider appearances.

SARAH Diplomatically speaking.

HUGH Are you laughing at me?

SARAH No, but I'm looking at you—just as though I had never seen you before.

> **LADY DEVON** *crosses centre and comes down between* **SARAH** *and* **HUGH**. **MRS MILLICK** *stands watching at right centre.*

ACT I, SCENE THREE

LADY DEVON Hugh, *dear*.

HUGH Yes, mother?

LADY DEVON I have been waiting for you downstairs. The carriage is at the door. Goodnight, Sarah.

SARAH Goodnight. I have been telling Hugh I was sorry to have behaved so badly.

LADY DEVON *(smiling)* I am afraid you're marrying a tomboy, Hugh.

SARAH No, no—I won't be one anymore.

LADY DEVON Dear child. *(She kisses her)* Come, Hugh. *(She moves over to* **MRS MILLICK***)*

HUGH Goodnight, Sarah.

SARAH Goodnight, Hugh.

HUGH starts to go right, then, recollecting himself, stops, turns to SARAH.

HUGH Will you drive with me tomorrow afternoon in Regent's Park?

SARAH Thank you—that will be delightful.

HUGH Until tomorrow—my dear.

He looks round carefully and then kisses her chastely on the forehead and departs with **LADY DEVON** *up right, after saying goodnight to* **MRS MILLICK***, who then crosses to right of* **SARAH** *at centre.* **SARAH** *has been gazing disappointedly after* **HUGH***.*

MRS MILLICK Well, that's over. Where are the girls?

SARAH Harriet and Gloria?

MRS MILLICK Yes.

SARAH Sitting out somewhere with Lord Edgar and Mr. Proutie.

MRS MILLICK And Effie and Jane and Honor and Victoria?

SARAH They're sitting out, too.

MRS. MILLICK Come with me—we must find them—really you modern young people have no sense of behaviour at all.

She goes with **SARAH** *into the supper room down left.*

When the stage is clear, **VICTORIA** *and* **LORD STEERE** *peep round the entrance down right.* **EFFIE** *and* **MR BETHEL** *do the same from the balcony up right.* **GLORIA** *and* **MR PROUTIE** *follow from balcony up right.* **HARRIET** *and* **LORD EDGAR JAMES**, **JANE** *and* **MR VALE**, **HONOR** *and* **LORD SORREL** *all follow from up left. The* **MEN** *form a line on right and the* **GIRLS** *form two lines on left, as they sing the first few lines. They should be in position by the time the* **MEN** *sing* ***"GENTLE AND SWEET"***. *As they sing they may do simple actions to suit the words interspersed with simple dance steps.*

"THE LAST DANCE"

MEN

THEY'VE ALL GONE NOW—HAVE NO FEAR—

GIRLS

SARAH'S MOTHER MAY BE NEAR,
IF SHE SHOULD HEAR

ALL

SHE MIGHT BE RATHER CROSS WITH US,
ELDERLY PEOPLE MAKE TOO MUCH FUSS.

MEN

ALWAYS INSIST ON A CHAPERONE,
NEVER LEAVE LOVE ALONE.

GIRLS

WE FEEL FRIGHTENED, IF YOU PLEASE
DON'T FLIRT OR TEASE.

MEN

GENTLE AND SWEET IN YOUR PURITY,
WE GIVE OUR HEARTS AS SECURITY.

GIRLS

WE SHALL BE SCOLDED A LOT FOR THIS.

MEN

YOU WON'T MISS JUST ONE KISS.

GIRLS *advance a pace or two and then retire.*

GIRLS

THINK OF THE CONSEQUENCES, PLEASE, YOU HAVEN'T REALIZED
WHAT AN APPALLING THING FOR US TO BE SO COMPROMISED,
SO DREADFULLY, DREADFULLY, DREADFULLY COMPROMISED.

MEN

EVERYTHING'S ENDING,
THE MOON IS DESCENDING,
BEHIND THE TALL TREES IN THE PARK.

GIRLS *curtsey.*

GIRLS

SILENCE FALLS,
SLUMBER CALLS.

MEN

WE MEN TOGETHER
WERE WONDERING WHETHER
WE MIGHT HAVE A BIT OF A LARK.

GIRLS *fan themselves.*

GIRLS

NO JOKES IN THE DARK, PLEASE,
WHAT SORT OF A LARK, PLEASE?

The **MEN** *advance a few paces and the* **GIRLS** *retreat.*

ALL

JUST A SLIGHT DANCE,
ONE MORE DREAM-OF-DELIGHT DANCE;
JUST A SORT OF GOODNIGHT DANCE
WOULD BE GLORIOUS FUN.

MEN

> WON'T YOU LET US, PLEASE LET US, JUST STAY FOR A WHILE?
> WON'T YOU, PLEASE WON'T YOU, BE GAY FOR A WHILE?
> ALL WE DESIRE IS TO PLAY FOR A WHILE
> NOW THE PARTY'S DONE.
>
> **MEN** *move back and the* **GIRLS** *forward to their original positions.*

ALL

> JUST A FAST WALTZ,
> TILL THE WORLD SEEMS A VAST WALTZ.
> VERY OFTEN THE LAST WALTZ
> IS THE BIRTH OF ROMANCE.
> IT'S A JUNE NIGHT,
> THERE'S A THRILL IN THE MOONLIGHT;
> LET'S GIVE WAY TO THE TENDER SURRENDER
> OF OUR LAST DANCE.

ALL

> JUST A SLIGHT DANCE,
> ONE MORE DREAM-OF-DELIGHT DANCE,
> JUST A SORT OF GOODNIGHT DANCE
> WOULD BE GLORIOUS FUN.

MEN

> WON'T YOU LET US, PLEASE LET US, JUST STAY FOR A WHILE?
> WON'T YOU, PLEASE WON'T YOU, BE GAY FOR A WHILE?
> ALL WE DESIRE IS TO PLAY FOR A WHILE
> NOW THE PARTY'S DONE.
>
> *During the following lines the* **GIRLS** *form one line on left and then come down front in a line across the footlights. The* **MEN** *come behind them and each one takes his own partner.*

ALL

> JUST A FAST WALTZ,
> TILL THE WORLD SEEMS A VAST WALTZ.
> VERY OFTEN THE LAST WALTZ

IS THE BIRTH OF ROMANCE.
IT'S A JUNE NIGHT,
THERE'S A THRILL IN THE MOONLIGHT;
LET'S GIVE WAY TO THE TENDER SURRENDER
OF OUR LAST DANCE.

They now waltz round the stage until the music cue for the following lines, when they sing as they dance.

GIRLS

AH! —

MEN

JUST A FAST WALTZ,
TILL THE WORLD SEEMS A VAST WALTZ.
VERY OFTEN THE LAST WALTZ
IS THE BIRTH OF ROMANCE.

ALL

IT'S A JUNE NIGHT,
THERE'S A THRILL IN THE MOONLIGHT;
LET'S GIVE WAY TO THE TENDER SURRENDER
OF OUR LAST DANCE.

During the music which follows they pantomime an alarm. The **MEN** *creep out up right with the exception of* **MR PROUTIE**, *who hides behind the column on the left of the stairs. The* **GIRLS** *take up the gilt chairs which stand round the walls and place them in a semicircle at centre. They then sit in them exactly at the last note of the music.*

Immediately after **MR. MILLICK** *enters from down left, followed by* **SARAH**. *She goes to the centre of the circle while* **SARAH** *stands at left.*

MRS MILLICK Girls—where have you been?

HARRIET Nowhere, Aunt Violet.

MRS MILLICK Where is Lord Edgar?

HONOR He went hours ago, Mrs Millick.

MRS MILLICK And Lord Steere, Mr Bethel, Mr Vale and Lord Sorrel?

VICTORIA *(sighing)* All gone.

MRS MILLICK And Mr Proutie? *(She goes upstage and looks at the stairs)*

GLORIA He was so tired he left early.

MRS MILLICK Come out from behind that pillar, Mr Proutie.

MR PROUTIE comes out, looking very sheepish. All the GIRLS giggle. He comes to centre above GLORIA's chair.

MR PROUTIE I—I—fell asleep—I apologize.

MRS MILLICK I quite understand.

MR PROUTIE *(appealingly to GLORIA)* Miss Gloria, I—

MR. MILLICK Goodnight, Mr Proutie.

MR PROUTIE Miss Gloria said that—

MRS MILLICK *(sternly)* Goodnight, Mr Proutie.

He comes down between GLORIA and HONOR and advances, clumsily to shake hands with MRS MILLICK. As he does so he bumps into GLORIA. He then backs into HONOR and finally makes a dive for the exit up right. He stops at the foot of the stairs, turns and speaks.

MR PROUTIE Er—er—goodnight—thank you for having me—er—goodnight.

He bows out up right.

MRS MILLICK Gloria—what does this mean?

GLORIA *(rising)* Nothing, Aunt Violet.

MRS MILLICK If it were not that this was a festive occasion, I should punish you severely for your deceit.

HARRIET *(rising and crossing to* **MRS MILLICK***)* Dear Aunt Violet—don't be cross.

MRS MILLICK To bed with the lot of you.

All **GIRLS** *rise and crowd round* **MRS MILLICK***.*

EFFIE Oh, not yet—just ten minutes more.

MRS MILLICK Certainly not—it's nearly one o'clock—fine bridesmaids you'll make on Thursday, if you stay up so late.

HARRIET Won't you let us stay up just a little longer?

HONOR Oh, Mrs Millick, do—please do.

MRS MILLICK No—Sarah's tired—

SARAH No, I'm not, mother—I know I couldn't sleep for ages.

GLORIA Just a short while—please!

MRS MILLICK *moves right.*

MRS MILLICK Very well—ten minutes then and no more. Sarah, come into my room and say goodnight.

SARAH Yes, mother.

MRS MILLICK *(at foot of stairs)* Remember now—in ten minutes' time I shall tell Parker to come and put out the lights—and don't make too much noise—

ALL We won't, we promise. Goodnight, Aunt Violet. Goodnight. Goodnight.

The **GIRLS** *wave to her as she goes upstairs. As soon as she has gone they fling aside their demure manner.* **EFFIE** *and* **HARRIET** *run to the piano and begin to strum. The other* **GIRLS** *put back the chairs.* **HONOR** *and* **GLORIA** *sit on the settee by the stairs with* **SARAH** *between them. All are laughing and talking,* **VICTORIA** *stands behind the settee,* **JANE** *sits on chair down left.* **EFFIE** *and* **HARRIET** *stop strumming and stand up left below the steps to the rostrum.*

HONOR Oh, Sarah—I do envy you—being married and going to Paris and everything.

SARAH Do you?

EFFIE Aren't you dying of excitement? —I know I should be.

SARAH No, not exactly—I feel strange somehow.

GLORIA What sort of strange?

SARAH I don't know—it's difficult to explain—perhaps I'm frightened.

JANE Nobody could be frightened of Hugh.

VICTORIA When I marry, it must be somebody just like Hugh.

HARRIET I shall choose someone smaller—more like myself, you know.

EFFIE How can you, Harriet—Hugh's just the right size.

GLORIA I shall marry Mr Proutie.

ALL Gloria! —What do you mean?

GLORIA *(calmly)* He adores me.

JANE Has he asked you?

GLORIA Of course.

HONOR And you said yes?

GLORIA I said no. But that doesn't matter—he'll ask me again.

EFFIE Are you in love with him?

GLORIA No—not a bit.

HONOR *(rises and moves down right)* How *can* you, Gloria?

GLORIA I'd much rather marry someone I didn't love really.

ALL "Gloria!" "Really!" "You're dreadful!" "Why?" *etc.*

GLORIA Because I could manage him better.

HARRIET I agree with Gloria.

VICTORIA So do I.

SARAH I don't—I want love.

EFFIE *(giggling)* So do I—but you'll get it before I do—

They all laugh.

HONOR I mean to have a lot of babies—

JANE I want someone to protect me always—someone strong that I can look up to—

HARRIET Fiddlesticks!

VICTORIA Old-fashioned nonsense!

GLORIA There's five minutes of our time gone already. Let's play a game.

SARAH What game?

EFFIE Yes, yes—any game.

HONOR Postman's knock.

SARAH No—no—that means one of us going out—

JANE How, when and where.

EFFIE So does that.

SARAH Let's play an exciting game—a noisy game.

All come down centre.

HARRIET Aunt Violet will hear.

SARAH No—she's two floors up.

GLORIA Blind Man's Buff.

All form a semicircle in the following order from right to left: **HONOR, SARAH, VICTORIA, GLORIA, HARRIET, JANE, EFFIE.**

EFFIE Yes—yes.

SARAH That will do—

VICTORIA Who'll be it—

JANE Eeny meeny miny mo—we must do eeny meeny miny mo—

Finale.

GLORIA
EENY MEENY MINY MO

HARRIET
CATCH A TIGER BY HIS TOE

VICTORIA
IF HE HOLLERS LET HIM GO

ALL
O-U-T SPELLS OUT AND SO

GLORIA
OUT GOES SHE. *(She points to* **EFFIE***)*

EFFIE
OUT GOES ME. THIS IS THE LOVELIEST, LOVELIEST PART OF THE PARTY. *(Sits on chair down left)*

GLORIA
EENY MEENY MINY MO

HARRIET
CATCH A TIGER BY HIS TOE

VICTORIA
IF HE HOLLERS LET HIM GO

ALL
O-U-T SPELLS OUT AND SO

VICTORIA }
SARAH   } OUT GOES SHE. *(***SARAH** *points to* **HARRIET***)*

HARRIET
OUT GOES ME.

> **EFFIE** *rises and she and* **HARRIET** *take hands and twirl around down left.*

HARRIET
EFFIE } NOW WE'RE FREE WHO KNOWS WHO'LL BE HE!

GLORIA
EENY MEENY MINY MO

VICTORIA
CATCH A TIGER BY HIS TOE

SARAH
IF HE HOLLERS LET HIM GO

JANE
VICTORIA
SARAH } O-U-T SPELLS OUT AND SO   **EFFIE**
GLORIA   **HARRIET** } WHO KNOWS WHO'LL BE "HE"?
HONOR

VICTORIA
OUT GOES SHE. *(She points to* **GLORIA***)*

GLORIA
OUT GOES ME. *(She joins* **EFFIE** *and* **HARRIET** *on left)*

ALL
THIS IS THE LOVELIEST, LOVELIEST PART OF THE PARTY.

VICTORIA
EENY MEENY MINY MO

SARAH
CATCH A TIGER BY HIS TOE

JANE
IF HE HOLLERS LET HIM GO
OUT GOES SHE. *(Points to* **VICTORIA***)*

VICTORIA
OUT GOES ME. *(She joins* **EFFIE**, **HARRIET** *and* **GLORIA** *on left)*

ALL
THIS IS THE LOVELIEST, LOVELIEST PART OF THE PARTY.

EFFIE ⎫ ONLY THREE OF THEM LEFT NOW, WE'RE EXCITED
HARRIET ⎭ TO SEE

GLORIA   ⎫ WHO IS GOING TO BE BLIND MAN, WHO'S IT GOING
VICTORIA ⎭ TO BE?

SARAH

I HAVE A STRANGE PRESENTIMENT IT'S ME.

JANE

EENY MEENY MINY MO
OUT GOES SHE. (*She points to* **HONOR**, *who joins the others on left*)

SARAH

EENY MEENY MO
OUT GOES SHE. (*She points to* **JANE**)
I'M HE—IT'S ME,
IT'S ME—I'M HE.

The **GIRLS** *move round behind* **SARAH** *at centre.*

GIRLS

JUST GET A HANDKERCHIEF AND BIND IT AROUND HER EYES,

SARAH

NOT TOO TIGHT, NOT TOO TIGHT.

EFFIE *comes centre and blindfolds her.*

GIRLS

SHE MUSTN'T SEE A THING, NO MATTER HOW MUCH SHE TRIES.

SARAH *pulls the handkerchief up over one eye.*

SARAH

THAT'S ALL RIGHT—THAT'S ALL RIGHT.

GIRLS

SHE WILL CHEAT IF SHE CAN,
THAT CORNER'S RAISED A BIT,
TURN HER ROUND TILL SHE'S DAZED A BIT.

ARE YOU READY NOW,
ONE, TWO, THREE!

EFFIE *turns her round. The others scatter,* **CARL** *enters from up right, puts his hat, scarf and coat on the settee up right centre, crosses to piano and starts to collect his music.*

SARAH

SINCE THE PARTY BEGAN,
SOMETHING'S BEEN TAUNTING ME,
SOME PRESENTIMENT HAUNTING ME,
WHAT CAN IT BE?

GIRLS

START NOW—START NOW,
SHE CAN SEE THE GROUND,
SHE CAN SEE THE GROUND.

SARAH

SOMEHOW, SOMEHOW,
SOME FORGOTTEN SOUND,
SOME FORGOTTEN SOUND,
ECHOES DEEP IN MY HEART,
STRANGELY ENTHRALLING ME,
SOMEONE SECRETLY CALLING ME,
LIKE A MELODY FAR AWAY.

GIRLS

OH, FOR HEAVEN'S SAKE START!
HERE, GO ALONG WITH YOU,
WE CAN SEE NOTHING WRONG WITH YOU,
WE WANT TO PLAY.

SARAH *pulls the bandage down over both eyes and starts to play.*

Lighting –Fade in blue floats to full.

They all dance about and dodge her.

CARL *picks up his music and is on his way out when* SARAH *clasps him round the neck at centre. All the* GIRLS *laugh.* CARL *is staggered for a moment, drops his music, and then completely losing all restraint kisses her on the mouth. She snatches the bandage from her eyes and stares into his face. All the other* GIRLS *are watching aghast. They should have reached the same approximate positions as at the beginning of the number.*

SARAH *(softly)* It's you I love—now and always.

She kisses him, then draws back and they stand there staring at one another oblivious of everything, EFFIE *giggles suddenly and then stops herself.*

HARRIET Sarah—

GLORIA Sarah—don't be silly—Sarah—

Neither CARL *nor* SARAH *turn their heads.*

CARL Come with me—

SARAH Now?

CARL Yes—now—tonight.

SARAH I'll come with you—wherever you want me to.

CARL I love you—do you hear?—I've loved you for months—for years really—ever since I was a boy I've known you were waiting for me somewhere—I'll take care of you—live for you—die for you.

SARAH Don't say that, my darling. *(Singing)*
SHOULD HAPPINESS FORSAKE ME.
AND DISILLUSION BREAK ME,
COME WHAT MAY,
LEAD THE WAY,
TAKE ME, TAKE ME.
ALTHOUGH I MAY DISCOVER,
LOVE CRUCIFIES THE LOVER,

WHATE'ER FATE HAS IN STORE,
MY HEART IS YOURS FOR EVERMORE.

CARL *(singing)*
OH LADY, YOU ARE FAR ABOVE ME,
AND YET YOU WHISPER THAT YOU LOVE ME.
CAN THIS BE TRUE OR IS IT JUST SOME FOOLISH DREAM?

SARAH *(speaking)* You know it's true, look in my eyes—can't you see?

CARL *(speaking softly)* Oh, my dear, dear love. *(He kisses her hand)*

Singing.
NOW THO' YOUR FEARS ARE SLEEPING,
LOOK WELL BEFORE THE LEAPING.
LOVE OF ME
MAY BE REPAID
BY WEEPING.
LIFE CAN BE BITTER LEARNING,
WHEN THERE IS NO RETURNING;
WHATE'ER FATE HAS IN STORE,
MY HEART IS YOURS FOR EVERMORE,
I LOVE YOU—I LOVE YOU—I LOVE YOU.

GLORIA *(coming down on left of* **CARL** *and tapping his shoulder with her fan)* You cannot realize the things you say.

You quite forget yourself, please go away.

HARRIET *(coming down on left of* **GLORIA***)* Now leave this all to me, my dear,

It's really too absurd.

EFFIE *(speaking from down left)* It's quite the most romantic thing that I have ever heard!

VICTORIA *(on right of* **SARAH***—speaking)* Effie, be quiet.

SARAH *kisses him again full on the mouth.* **HARRIET** *drags them apart.*

HARRIET Sarah—are you mad? —Mr Linden, please go at once.

CARL (*smiling*) How can I go?

GLORIA Harriet—leave this to me—

SARAH Stop—don't say another word.

EFFIE (*hysterically*) It's the most wonderfully thrilling thing that ever happened in the world.

HARRIET Don't be an idiot, Effie.

SARAH (*quietly*) Effie's right, Harriet.

HARRIET I'm going straight upstairs to fetch Aunt Violet.

Goes right to stairs, **EFFIE** *rushes across and holds her back as she gets to the bottom step.*

EFFIE (*struggling with her*) You shan't! You shan't! —They love each other—look at them—Honor, Victoria, Jane, help me

HONOR, **VICTORIA** *and* **JANE** *come to her assistance and bring her down stage right.*

SARAH AND CARL (*singing*)
  I'LL SEE YOU AGAIN,
  WHENEVER SPRING BREAKS THROUGH AGAIN,
  ALWAYS I'LL BE BY YOUR SIDE,
  NO TIME OR TIDE
  CAN PART US EVER—

VICTORIA Shhh! Someone's coming—hide—quickly—

They all hide quickly, **SARAH**, **HONOR** *and* **VICTORIA** *behind left column of stairs,* **GLORIA** *and* **JANE** *outside on balcony left.* **HARRIET** *picks up the music dropped by* **CARL** *and goes outside on balcony right.* **EFFIE** *behind right column of stairs,* **CARL** *behind settee up right centre.*

As soon as they are hidden, four pompous **FOOTMEN**, *holding long poles for turning out the gas, in their left*

hands, enter in single file from down right. They march solemnly to centre, where they turn front in line.

FOOTMEN *Quartette.*
NOW THE PARTY'S REALLY ENDED,
AND OUR BETTERS HAVE ASCENDED,
ALL WITH THROBBING HEADS,
TO THEIR WELCOME BEDS,
PITY US, WHO HAVE TO BE UP,
SADLY CLEARING THE DEBRIS UP,
GETTING FOR OUR PAINS
MOST OF THE REMAINS.
THOUGH THE MAJOR-DOMO IS A TRIFLE TIGHT,
THOUGH THE MISTRESS HICCOUGHED WHEN SHE SAID GOOD NIGHT,
WE, IN OUR SECLUDED GARRET,
MEAN TO FINISH UP THE CLARET –
CUP ALL RIGHT.
WHEN WE'VE DOUSED THE FINAL CANDLES,
WE'LL DISCUSS THE LATEST SCANDALS
WE HAVE OVERHEARD,
PLEASURE LONG DEFERRED.
WHEN THE DUKE OF SO AND SO STARES
AT HIS WIFE, WE KNOW BELOW STAIRS,
WHILE SHE SMIRKS AND STRUTS,
THAT HE HATES HER GUTS.
THOUGH WE ALL DISGUISE OUR FEELINGS PRETTY WELL,
WHAT WE MEAN BY "VERY GOOD " IS "GO TO HELL."
THOUGH THEY'RE ALL SO GRAND AND POMPOUS,
MOST OF THEM ARE NOW NON COMPOS,
SERVE THEM RIGHT.

They turn up stage and put out the gas lamps with their poles, then exit in line down right as they finish singing.

Lighting – black out everything except blue floats and backcloth lighting, as **FOOTMEN** *turn the gas out.*
GOODNIGHT. GOODNIGHT. GOODNIGHT.

The **GIRLS** *peep out to see if the coast is clear.* **CARL** *and* **SARAH** *come down to left centre.* **VICTORIA** *and* **GLORIA** *go off down right and left respectively and each bring in a lighted candle.*

Lighting – bring up special blue spot and one front-of-house white arc.

The **GIRLS** *all group round* **CARL** *and* **SARAH** *with* **VICTORIA** *and* **GLORIA** *down stage right and left of the group.*

GIRLS
THEY'VE ALL GONE NOW—HAVE NO FEAR—

CARL
SARAH'S MOTHER MAY BE NEAR,
IF SHE SHOULD HEAR

ALL
SHE MIGHT BE RATHER CROSS WITH US,
ELDERLY PEOPLE MAKE TOO MUCH FUSS.
ALWAYS INSIST ON A CHAPERONE;
NEVER LEAVE LOVE ALONE.

SARAH
I FEEL FRIGHTENED. OH, MY DEAR,
PLEASE CALM MY FEAR.

CARL
GENTLE AND SWEET IN YOUR PURITY,
I GIVE MY HEART AS SECURITY.
I SHALL BE LIVING MY LIFE ANEW,
LOVING YOU—LOVING YOU.

GIRLS
THINK OF THE CONSEQUENCES, PLEASE, YOU HAVEN'T REALIZED
WHAT AN APPALLING THING FOR YOU TO BE SO COMPROMISED,
SO DREADFULLY, DREADFULLY, DREADFULLY COMPROMISED.

SARAH *(speaking)* Harriet—whatever you do won't be the slightest use—I love Carl—I'm going with him—I don't care where or how—but this is my life, you understand—my whole life—so help me—all you can—please—please—

GLORIA Think of Hugh—Sarah, you're mad.

SARAH Perhaps I am mad, but I'm happy—can't you see? —I'm really happy—

HARRIET Mr Linden, I appeal to you.

GLORIA It's no use, Harriet.

HARRIET I feel as if I were in a dream.

CARL You are.

HARRIET What are your prospects?—have you any money?

CARL None—no money—but I can earn enough.

SARAH So can I—I'll sing—

VICTORIA Sarah!

CARL Yes—Sarah will sing and I will play and we will make a living—come, Sarah.

SARAH Like this?

EFFIE Quickly, Gloria—your bedroom is nearest—your hat and cape.

> **GLORIA** *puts her candle on table down left and she and* **EFFIE** *fly upstairs.* **CARL** *gets his hat, coat and scarf from settee, puts them on and goes to centre where he meets* **SARAH**. *The* **GIRLS** *remain at left centre.*

SARAH AND CARL *(singing)*
FLING FAR BEHIND YOU
THE CHAINS THAT BIND YOU,
THAT LOVE MAY FIND YOU
IN JOY OR STRIFE;
THO' FATE MAY CHEAT YOU,
AND DEFEAT YOU,

YOUR YOUTH MUST ANSWER TO THE CALL OF LIFE.
THERE IS A—

EFFIE *and* **GLORIA** *come downstairs with a hat and cape which they put on* **SARAH**. *She and* **CARL** *exit slowly through the arch down right.* **EFFIE** *sits on a chair down right and cries. The other* **GIRLS** *look after them and wave.*

The curtain is lowered as **CARL** *and* **SARAH** *get to the door.*

Lighting – front-of-house arc and floats out.

First Interval

ACT II

Scene One

The Interior of **HERR SCHLICK**'s *Café in Vienna in 1880.*

The time is 12 noon.

The set consists of a bandstand in the middle where **CARL** *is rehearsing his orchestra, consisting of a pianist at an old-fashioned upright piano, a violinist and a third who can be playing a large piano accordion,* **CARL** *himself plays a violin. He is in his shirt-sleeves; his coat is on the piano. At the back is a rostrum running right across the stage (this can be doubled from ACT I, Scene Three), having tables and chairs grouped on it. Behind this is the wall which has a street door at right centre and a window at left centre. Both look out on to the street. There is another rostrum on the right, but this may be dispensed with if desired and the tables and chairs set on the stage level. Down right is a large table with chairs and a plush settee and a similar table with chairs and settee is down left. There are entrances down left and up right and left. There is a large stove above the down right entrance and a table below the bandstand at centre. The whole place is in disorder as the cleaners, etc., are cleaning it for the evening. Most of the chairs are upside down on the tables, and several of the tables are out of place while the sweeping is going on. The place is gaudy and lit (in next scene) by many gas globes.*

Lighting – floats white at 1/4. Floats blue at full. Battens blue at 1/2. Lengths, spots and floods as required. Fittings out.

The curtain rises at music cue. The stage band plays with the orchestra for a few bars and then **CARL** *stops them. He sips a cup of coffee and looks over his music while the other members of the band read newspapers and chat.* **WAITERS** *in their shirt-sleeves,* **CLEANERS** *and* **CHARWOMEN** *are cleaning and polishing as they sing the opening number.* **LOTTE**, **HANSI** *and* **FREDA**, *three ladies of the town, are sitting at the table down right.* **LOTTE** *is on left of table,* **FREDA** *is up stage and* **HANSI** *is on right of it. Two* **WAITERS** *take a table which has been set right down stage centre and put it at the back near the window. The* **CLEANERS** *set the other tables and chairs in the position they should be in for ACT II, Scene Two.*

WAITERS
LIFE IN THE MORNING ISN'T TOO BRIGHT,
WHEN YOU'VE HAD TO HURRY ROUND AND CARRY PLATES
   ALL NIGHT;
AND THE EVENING ISN'T TOO GAY,
WHEN YOU KNOW YOU'VE GOT TO RISE AND BE AT WORK ALL
   DAY.
THIS CAFÉ MERELY CATERS
FOR A HORDE OF DRUNKEN SATYRS,
WHY, OH WHY, WE'RE WAITERS NOBODY CAN SAY.

WAITERS
LIFE IN THE MORNING ISN'T TOO BRIGHT,
WHEN YOU'VE HAD TO HURRY ROUND AND CARRY
   PLATES ALL NIGHT.

CLEANERS
OH DEAR, IT'S CLEAR TO SEE THAT CLEANERS
   LEAD A WORSE LIFE.

WAITERS
AND THE EVENING ISN'T TOO GAY,
WHEN YOU KNOW YOU'VE GOT TO RISE AND BE AT
   WORK ALL DAY.

CLEANERS
YOU SEE THE REASON WHY EACH DAY WE WANT
   TO CURSE LIFE

ACT II, SCENE ONE

The **WAITERS, CLEANERS** *and* **CHARWOMEN** *start to move to the back and exit up right and left, gradually leaving the stage clear except for the band and* **LOTTE**, **FREDA** *and* **HANSI**, *who remain at the table down right. The others sing as they go.*

Lighting – bring white floats up to 3/4.

WAITERS / CLEANERS FOR THIS CAFÉ MERELY CATERS WEARY

WAITERS / CLEANERS FOR A HORDE OF DRUNKEN SATYRS; DREARY

WAITERS / CLEANERS WHY, OH WHY, WE'RE WAITERS NOBODY CAN SAY. EVERY DAY.

WAITERS / CLEANERS AH—AH—AH— AH—AH—AH—

LOTTE He left me at half-past ten, my dear, he kissed my hand, à la grand chevalier, which made me laugh, I *must* say.

FREDA Is that all he left you with—a kiss?

LOTTE Don't be vulgar, Freda, everything was arranged last night in his carriage—we drove round and round the Ringstrasse.

HANSI I hope it didn't make you too giddy, dear.

LOTTE You none of you understand, this is an "affaire de coeur", I'm sure of it.

*ic*FRITZ, *a waiter, enters from up right and brings* **LOTTE** *a bill for the coffee and brioches they have been having.*

It's not my turn—Hansi?

HANSI I paid yesterday.

FREDA *searches for money in her stocking.*

LOTTE Come along, Freda—no fumbling.

FREDA I wasn't fumbling—I was just trying to count up how many times I've paid during the last month.

HANSI That oughtn't to take you long.

FREDA *(rather crossly)* Oh, here you are, then. *(She gives him some money and he exits up right)*

LOTTE Where was I?

FREDA Driving round the Ringstrasse, my dear, talking business.

LOTTE You can all jeer if you like, but just you wait and see. Anyhow, I feel positively exhausted, having had to get up so early.

HANSI I'm tired too.

> GUSSI *enters from street, elaborately dressed and wearing a fur tippet and muff. She comes down centre.*

GUSSI Hallo, girls!

> HANSI *rises and goes to right of* GUSSI.

FREDA Oh, my God, look at Gussi!

HANSI *(fingering the tippet)* Where did you get it?

GUSSI Here, leave off, surely you've seen a bit of mink before?

HANSI Not on you, I haven't.

GUSSI Well, have a good look now and enjoy it.

LOTTE Who gave it to you?

GUSSI *(with great coyness)* I hardly like to tell you, it was such a delightful surprise—I had been spending the night with my dear old grandmother—

HANSI I hope she took her spurs off.

> LOTTE *and* FREDA *laugh,* HANSI *goes back to her seat,* GUSSI *crosses right and sits down stage of* HANSI.

LOTTE Do you want some coffee?

GUSSI No thanks, it would spoil my lunch.

FREDA I'm lunching at Sacher's—I can bring a friend—Hansi?

HANSI No thank you, dear.

FREDA Lotte?

LOTTE Who are you lunching with, the old ostrich?

FREDA No, he's gone to Warsaw. This is a banker—quite young, but common, no use for dinner—do you want to come?

LOTTE I don't mind.

HANSI I can't imagine, Freda, why you waste your time with small fry.

FREDA I don't consider any free meal small fry.

HANSI Where's the Snow Queen?

LOTTE Sari?

HANSI Yes.

LOTTE She'll be here soon, looking at Carl with sheep's eyes.

GUSSI Don't laugh at her, she does adore him.

LOTTE It's all very well to adore your husband, dear, but silly to overdo it.

FREDA Whenever any of the officers ask her to dance, she goes off into a decline.

HANSI There's no doubt about it, love is very bad for business.

> **HANSI, FREDA, GUSSI** *and* **LOTTE** *all rise and go centre (in that order from right to left), where they stand in line across the footlights and begin their number. All start with their hands on their hips and sing throughout with great spirit. From time to time, suitable actions can be made in unison.*
>
> ### *"LADIES OF THE TOWN"*
>
> THOUGH WE'RE OFTEN ACCUSED OF EXCESSIVELY PLASTIC,
>   DRASTIC SINS,
> WHEN WE'RE ASKED TO DECIDE ON THE WRONG OR THE
>   RIGHT LIFE,

NIGHT LIFE WINS,
WE KNOW THAT DESTINY WILL NEVER BRING
A WEDDING RING ABOUT.
OUR MORAL SENSE MAY REALLY NOT BE QUITE THE THING
TO FLING ABOUT, SING ABOUT;
WE'LL ACHIEVE INDEPENDENCE BEFORE IT'S TOO LATE, AND
WAIT AND SEE.
WHAT CARE, WHAT CARE WE?

They all move left with a swinging motion of the hips.

Refrain.

LADIES OF THE TOWN, LADIES OF THE TOWN,
THOUGH WE'VE NOT A CONFESSIONAL AIR,
WE HAVE QUITE A PROFESSIONAL FLAIR,

They flaunt right.

STROLLING UP AND DOWN, STROLLING UP AND DOWN,
WE EMPLOY QUITE AN AMIABLE SYSTEM
OF ACHIEVING RENOWN,
THOUGH THE CHURCH AND STATE ABUSES US,
FOR AS LONG AS IT AMUSES US,

Cross back to centre.

WE'LL REMAIN, NO MATTER HOW THEY FROWN,
HAUGHTY, NAUGHTY, LADIES OF THE TOWN.

All turn up stage, go up a few paces and shake their bustles, turn front and come down stage for the next verse.

WE CAN OFTEN BEHAVE IN A VERY DISARMING, CHARMING
  WAY.

All pretend to put money in their stockings.

WHICH CAN FREQUENTLY ADD TO THE MONEY WE LAY BY,
DAY BY DAY.
IF WE ARE TOLD OF SOMETHING ON THE STOCK EXCHANGE,
WE PRY A BIT,
AND IF IT'S SAFE WE GET SOME KINDLY BANKER

TO SUPPLY A BIT, BUY A BIT,
AND IF LATER OUR HELPERS MAY WISH TO FORGET US
SET US FREE,

All put their right hands up in an attitude of devil-may-care.

WHAT CARE, WHAT CARE WE?

All move right with a swinging motion of the hips.

Refrain.

LADIES OF THE TOWN, LADIES OF THE TOWN,
THOUGH WE'RE SOCIALLY UNDER A CLOUD,
PLEASE FORGIVE US FOR LAUGHING ALOUD,

All flaunt left.

STROLLING UP AND DOWN, STROLLING UP AND DOWN,
DISAPPROVAL MAY SOMETIMES SUBMERGE US,
BUT WE NONE OF US DROWN.
WE HAVE KNOWN IN GREAT VARIETY
MEMBERS OF THE BEST SOCIETY,
AND SHOULD WE DECIDE TO SETTLE DOWN,
WE'LL BE WEALTHY LADIES OF THE TOWN.

They pull their handkerchiefs out of their left sleeves and carefully drop them on the stone. Then they pantomime the action of watching a man go by, hoping he will pick them up. He doesn't, so they pick them up themselves and put them back in their sleeves. They then dance some simple steps, making the most of their bustles.

WHEN WE MEET THE ROYAL PRINCES,
IT'S RATHER SWEET HOW EACH ONE WINCES.
UNEASY LIES THE HEAD THAT WEARS A CROWN
ALL BECAUSE OF LADIES OF THE TOWN.

Then all march off down left, giving a final flick to their bustles as they exit. When **LOTTE**, **FREDA** *and* **HANSI** *have gone off* **CARL** *addresses his band.*

CARL Boys, when you take the first refrain, bring it out, let it live and breathe, and mean something. In the last four bars I've marked a rallentando—Now then—

He raises his baton and the stage band begins **"BONNE NUIT, MERCI"** *—as the music swells* MANON *enters briskly from the street and comes down centre; she listens for a moment, and then stamps her foot.* CARL *stops the band.*

MANON No, Carl—it must be quicker there.

CARL When we were rehearsing yesterday that was the exact spot you wanted it slower.

MANON Listen—it starts so— *(She sings)*

"Lorsque j'étais petite fille en marchant parmi les prés" —swift, staccato like that, then "J'entendis la voix d'ma tante, qui MURMURAIT à côté"

—just a leetle slower—not very much, you understand—

She removes her hat and coat and puts them on the table down right.

CARL Very well. *(He starts the music again, very fast. After a few bars he stops)* How's that?

MANON *(she bangs the chair on left of table on the stage)* No, no, no—you are so stubborn.

CARL Stubborn? *(He vaults the rail in front of the bandstand and comes to left of her)*

MANON *(sitting on table)* Yes—you are a musician, yes, but you know nothing about singers, especially when they have no voice like me.

CARL You have a beautiful voice, Manon.

MANON *(laughing suddenly)* Now you are being earnest and sincere, it is so many years since I saw that solemn look in your eyes—

ACT II, SCENE ONE

CARL You can't expect me to pay you compliments often, when you try to quarrel with me all the time.

MANON I quarrel! Don't be a fool.

CARL *(turning away)* It's you who are a fool— *(moves to centre)*

MANON *(rising, following him and touching his arm, softly)* No, Carl—I was once—but I'm not any more.

CARL What do you mean?

MANON Where is Sari—your little English Sarah?

CARL She will be here soon.

MANON *(mockingly)* How exciting! *(She goes right a little)*

CARL You do hate her, don't you?

MANON *(gaily)* Passionately *(she goes back to him at centre)* —I should like to scratch her eyes out and pull her nose off and wring her neck—

CARL Manon!

MANON —in a friendly way. *(She laughs again and moves away right)*

CARL *(he goes to the chair which is on the right of the centre table, puts his foot on it and buttons his boot)* Don't laugh like that.

MANON You used to love my laughter—it was so gay and charming, you said—I think you mentioned once that it reminded you of a bird chirruping, that was a very pretty thought, Carl—

As he is still bending over, doing up his boot, she smacks his stern and runs up towards the street door. He follows.

CARL Please go away now—I must continue my rehearsal.

MANON Carl—

They return laughing to down centre. He then jumps back over the rail to the bandstand.

CARL Yes.

MANON *(going up to column on right of bandstand)* I'm only teasing you and irritating you because I'm jealous—

CARL But, Manon—

MANON *(holding up her hand)* No, don't protest and say I have no right to be jealous! *(She crosses to table down right)* I know that well—ours was such a silly little affair really, and so long ago, but somehow it was very sweet and it left a small sting behind—here *(indicates her heart)*.

CARL It was your fault that it ended.

MANON I know that too *(she sits on table)* —and I'm glad—I was very proud of myself finishing it all suddenly like that *(smacks her hands together)* —because it was for the best— I'm no good for you really—not faithful enough, and you should be free always, because you're an artist. But now you'll never be free, so my beautiful little sacrifice was all in vain. *(She laughs)* Go back to your work—I'll run through my words here—

CARL But, Manon, you can't—

MANON Please—play my music for me—I'm not sure of it yet— I'm not sure of anything.

> **CARL** *looks at her silently for a moment, and then turns to his band.* **MANON** *calls* "**FRITZ**" *and a* **WAITER** *enters from up right and comes down to her with a glass of Viennese coffee with two straws, which he hands to her.*

FRITZ Bonjour, Madame.

MANON Ah! Bonjour, Fritz. Vous ne l'avez pas oublié ce matin, n'est-ce pas?

FRITZ Non, Madame, pas oublier, jamais.

MANON Comment ça va?

FRITZ Très bien, Madame, et vous?

MANON Très bien; et votre femme?

FRITZ Très bien.

MANON Et le petit bébé?

FRITZ Ah! Le petit bébé, il est aussi beau que son papa!

>**MANON** *pays him.*

>Merci bien, Madame. *(He exits up right)*

MANON Bon garçon, Fritz.

>*Then, still sitting on the table and occasionally sucking her coffee through the straws, she sings her number.*

>**"IF LOVE WERE ALL"**

LIFE IS VERY ROUGH AND TUMBLE,
FOR A HUMBLE
DISEUSE,
ONE CAN BETRAY ONE'S TROUBLES NEVER,
WHATEVER
OCCURS,
NIGHT AFTER NIGHT,
HAVE TO LOOK BRIGHT,
WHETHER YOU'RE WELL OR ILL
PEOPLE MUST LAUGH THEIR FILL.
YOU MUSTN'T SLEEP
TILL DAWN COMES CREEPING.
THOUGH I NEVER REALLY GRUMBLE
LIFE'S A JUMBLE.
INDEED—
AND IN MY EFFORTS TO SUCCEED
I'VE HAD TO FORMULATE A CREED—

>*Refrain.*

I BELIEVE IN DOING WHAT I CAN,
IN CRYING WHEN I MUST,
IN LAUGHING WHEN I CHOOSE.
HEIGH-HO, IF LOVE WERE ALL
I SHOULD BE LONELY.
I BELIEVE THE MORE YOU LOVE A MAN,

THE MORE YOU GIVE YOUR TRUST,
THE MORE YOU'RE BOUND TO LOSE.
ALTHOUGH WHEN SHADOWS FALL
I THINK IF ONLY—

She looks at **CARL**.

SOMEBODY SPLENDID REALLY NEEDED ME,
SOMEONE AFFECTIONATE AND DEAR,
CARES WOULD BE ENDED IF I KNEW THAT HE
WANTED TO HAVE ME NEAR.
BUT I BELIEVE THAT SINCE MY LIFE BEGAN
THE MOST I'VE HAD IS JUST
A TALENT TO AMUSE.
HEIGH-HO, IF LOVE WERE ALL!

THO' LIFE BUFFETS ME OBSCENELY,
IT SERENELY
GOES ON.
ALTHOUGH I QUESTION ITS CONCLUSION,
ILLUSION
IS GONE.
FREQUENTLY I
PUT A BIT BY
SAFE FOR A RAINY DAY.
NOBODY HERE CAN SAY
TO WHAT, INDEED,
THE YEARS ARE LEADING.
FATE MAY OFTEN TREAT ME MEANLY,
BUT I KEENLY
PURSUE
A LITTLE MIRAGE IN THE BLUE.
DETERMINATION HELPS ME THROUGH.

2nd refrain.

I BELIEVE IN DOING WHAT I CAN,
IN CRYING WHEN I MUST,
IN LAUGHING WHEN I CHOOSE.
HEIGH-HO, IF LOVE WERE ALL
I SHOULD BE LONELY.

I BELIEVE THE MORE YOU LOVE A MAN,
THE MORE YOU GIVE YOUR TRUST,
THE MORE YOU'RE BOUND TO LOSE.
ALTHOUGH WHEN SHADOWS FALL
I THINK IF ONLY—

She looks at CARL *again.*

SOMEBODY SPLENDID REALLY NEEDED ME,
SOMEONE AFFECTIONATE AND DEAR,
CARES WOULD BE ENDED IF I KNEW THAT HE
WANTED TO HAVE ME NEAR.
BUT I BELIEVE THAT SINCE MY LIFE BEGAN
THE MOST I'VE HAD IS JUST
A TALENT TO AMUSE.
HEIGH-HO. IF LOVE WERE ALL!

She crosses to the table below bandstand and sits left of it with her head on her hand, CARL *and his band strike up **"BONNE NUIT, MERCI"**.* MANON *taps out the time on the table.*

Un, deux, trois; un, deux, trois. Mon cher ami, toute à l'heure c'était encore trop vite! Trop vite!

CARL Mais je ne veux pas jouer plus lentement, c'est le bon rythme. Il m'est impossible de le changer.

MANON *(rising and facing him)* Sapristi, il n'y a rien d'impossible, tu es toujours embêté.

CARL Fiche-moi la paix ! Tu m'embêtes toute la journée. Tu m'embêtes. Tu ne connais pas ton métier. Puisque je t'ai dit que tu as une jolie voix, tu crois que tu es une grande artiste.

MANON Mais non, mais non. Jamais de la vie! Crois-tu que parce que tu as épousé cette petite anglaise de rien du tout, que tu peux te donner de grands airs.

CARL Ça ne te regarde pas à qui je suis marié ou pas. Ça, c'est mon affaire. Manon, Manon, sois tranquille, ne sois pas fâchée, terminons la chanson.

MANON Ah non, je ne suis pas vraiment fâchée.

Sings.
I THINK IF SOMEBODY SPLENDID REALLY NEEDED ME,
SOMEONE AFFECTIONATE AND DEAR,
CARES WOULD BE ENDED IF I KNEW THAT HE
WANTED TO HAVE ME NEAR.
BUT I BELIEVE THAT SINCE MY LIFE BEGAN
THE MOST I'VE HAD IS JUST
A TALENT TO AMUSE.
HEIGH-HO, IF LOVE WERE ALL!

She exits down left. **CARL** *dismisses his band, who go out through the street door up right centre, and then he jumps over the bandstand rail and puts his coat on at centre.* **GUSSI** *enters from down left and comes to left of him.*

GUSSI Hallo, Carl.

CARL *(absently)* Hallo.

GUSSI Like a drink?

CARL No, thanks.

GUSSI Are you lunching with anyone?

CARL Yes, my wife.

GUSSI I might have known it. *(She slips her arm through his)* Let me know when you feel like being unfaithful to her, won't you?

CARL *(smiling)* You're bad, Gussi. *(He moves over right)* Thoroughly bad—go along with you.

GUSSI Here, listen: you know that dark red coat of mine?

CARL *(coming back to centre)* Yes.

GUSSI Would your Sari like it? I've had this given to me. *(She waves her muff)* I shan't need it any more.

CARL It's very, very sweet of you, Gussi.

GUSSI You both look so pinched—it depresses me to look at you—bring Sarah along to lunch at my flat—

CARL Very well.

> **CAPTAIN AUGUST LUTTE** *enters from street door up right centre. As he comes down to centre.* **GUSSI** *takes hold of* **CARL** *and pushes him towards the door down left. The* **CAPTAIN** *goes to right of table below bandstand.*

GUSSI Just a moment, some good news has come in—come at one-thirty, if I'm not back tell Liza to serve you.

CARL But, Gussi—

GUSSI *(firmly)* Goodbye, dear Carl—

> **CARL** *goes off laughing down left.*

> **GUSSI** *sidles up to* **CAPTAIN AUGUST LUTTE**.

Good morning.

CAPTAIN *(bowing stiffly)* Good morning.

GUSSI Can I do anything for you?

CAPTAIN I wish to see Herr Schlick.

GUSSI *(grimacing)* How nice!

CAPTAIN *(abruptly)* You are very pretty.

GUSSI *(pretending to faint)* Oh, Captain—my salts—my salts.

CAPTAIN Perhaps you will make a rendezvous with me for next week?

GUSSI I may be dead next week, what's the matter with now?

CAPTAIN I fear that I am otherwise engaged.

> **HERR SCHLICK** *enters, oily and ingratiating, from down left and comes between the* **CAPTAIN** *and* **GUSSI**.

HERR SCHLICK Captain—forgive me, please—I— *(Sees* **GUSSI***)* What are you doing here?

GUSSI Just feeding the swans—Goodbye, one and all. Goodbye.

She goes off through street door.

CAPTAIN Herr Schlick, I have a complaint to make.

HERR SCHLICK It shall be rectified—before you say it, whatever is wrong is rectified.

CAPTAIN Among your professional dancing partners you have been careless enough to engage an iceberg.

HERR SCHLICK Good God!

MANON enters from up left and crosses behind bandstand, goes quietly to table down right and gets her hat and coat. The others do not see her.

CAPTAIN A beautiful, alluring, unsociable iceberg—her name is Sari.

HERR SCHLICK She is new, Captain; she has only been here a few weeks.

CAPTAIN Even a few weeks is surely time enough to enable her to melt sufficiently to sup with me—

HERR SCHLICK She is English, Captain, one must make allowances.

CAPTAIN I do not come to a café of this sort to make allowances—I come to amuse myself and to pay for it.

HERR SCHLICK *(very flurried)* Captain—I assure you—anything that you wish—I will arrange as soon as possible.

CAPTAIN I wish for this Sari to sup with me—tonight.

HERR SCHLICK She shall, Captain, she shall.

CAPTAIN You will please have a special supper laid ready in a quiet room—Number Seven is the best, I think—

By this time MANON has heard that they are talking about SARI and creeps over left behind bandstand and hides behind it on the left. She listens intently.

HERR SCHLICK You are sure that you would not rather have Lotte or perhaps Hansi—

CAPTAIN Quite sure.

HERR SCHLICK You see this English girl is the wife of my orchestra leader—they are said to be in love—it will be a little difficult—

CAPTAIN I hope I have made myself quite clear—

> **SARI** *comes in from the street door and comes straight down to table right.*

HERR SCHLICK But, Captain—

CAPTAIN You will please arrange things as I have suggested—tonight I wish no allowances to be made. *(He turns and sees* **SARI**, *clicks his heels and bows)* Good morning.

SARI Good morning.

CAPTAIN It is a beautiful morning.

SARI Beautiful.

CAPTAIN But chilly.

SARI It is very warm outside. *(She takes off her hat, coat and gloves and puts them on the table beside her)*

CAPTAIN Would you honour me by lunching with me?

SARI I'm so sorry, but I am already engaged.

CAPTAIN Perhaps a drive a little later on; we might go up to Cobenzil—

SARI Please forgive me, but today it is impossible.

CAPTAIN I am expecting you to have supper with me tosnight.

SARI Thank you very much, but I'm afraid I have another appointment.

CAPTAIN We shall see.

He bows again and exits through the street door, SCHLICK *crosses to left of* SARI, *furiously.*

HERR SCHLICK It may interest you to know that you are losing me one of my most valued clients—

SARI *blows into one of her gloves so that it flies into* SCHLICK's *face.*

I'll deal with you later. Captain—a moment, please—Captain—

He rushes off after the CAPTAIN, SARI *looks after him pensively for a moment and then sighs,* MANON *comes down to centre, where she meets* SARI, *who is crossing left.*

MANON Sari.

SARI Oh!

MANON Don't look so startled—

SARI I came to find Carl. *(She crosses in front of* MANON *as though to go out left, then stops and turns to her)* Have you seen him?

MANON Yes, I've just been rehearsing with him. *(Going to right centre)*

SARI Oh!

MANON He's about somewhere.

SARI I'll find him. *(She turns to go)*

MANON I want to speak to you.

SARI *(coldly, as she stops and turns to* MANON *again)* Yes? What is it?

MANON Oh, why do you always look at me like that?

SARI Like what?

MANON Aloof and superior

SARI I wasn't conscious of being either of those things.

ACT II, SCENE ONE

MANON Yes, you were—you know you were—you always are with me. But, listen, never mind about that now—I heard Schlick arranging for you to have supper in a private room with Captain August tonight.

SARI What! *(Going anxiously to left of MANON)*

MANON So be careful.

SARI *(incredulously)* You heard Schlick arranging for *me*—

MANON Yes—yes, yes—I thought you might like to know.

SARI How horrible!

MANON Not so horrible as all that; lots of the girls here would be glad of the chance, but as Carl is in love with you and you are apparently in love with him, I thought—

SARI *(rather stiffly)* Thank you, Manon.

MANON Not at all. *(She turns to go out of street door)*

SARI Manon—

MANON *(stopping)* Yes?

SARI I'm sorry.

MANON What for?

SARI If my manner is—well, unkind—

MANON *(patting her arm)* Ça ne fait rien, ma chère—I don't love him any more, really, at least I don't think I do, and anyhow you have no reason to be jealous, nothing to be afraid of. Look at me, and then look in the glass. *(She kisses her lightly, and goes off humming a reprise of **"BONNE NUIT, MERCI"**, as she passes out of the street door)*

SARI goes to table down right and sits on left of it in the chair. She puts her head down on her arms, sobbing "Carl! Carl!".

CARL enters from down left with his overcoat and hat on his arm and, seeing SARI, puts his hat and coat on the table down left and crosses straight over to her and puts his arm round her.

SARI Carl!

CARL Darling! *(He kisses her fondly)* How quick you've been dressing! I crept out without waking you.

SARI Yes, I know; you must never do that again.

CARL Why—what's the matter?

SARI *(rising)* I dreamt—something dreadful. I awoke terrified—I came straight here without any coffee or anything—to see if you were safe.

CARL I safe? Why, of course I'm safe—why shouldn't I be? What could have happened to me? Don't be silly.

SARI I don't know, I'm frightened. I hate this place—let's go away.

They start to sing, in each other's arms.

DUET: "EVERMORE AND A DAY"

SARI *and* **CARL**.

CARL

WHY ARE YOU WEEPING, DEAR?
WHAT SHADOW HAUNTED YOU IN SLEEPING, DEAR?
THO' PORTENTS AND FEARS
YOUR COURAGE MAY BE PLUNDERING,
YOUR FAITH IN MY LOVE
SHOULD LEAVE NO TIME FOR WONDERING.
EVER YOUR DREAMS ARE IN MY KEEPING, DEAR.

CARL *kneels.*

SARI

AH! NO! MY SWEET,
FATE KNOWS OUR HAPPINESS IS TOO COMPLETE.
THO' NOW IN OUR LOVE'S SECURITY
WE LIVE AWHILE,

ACT II, SCENE ONE

A LITTLE OF HEART'S CONTENT
THE GODS MAY GIVE AWHILE,

SARI *crosses to centre.* **CARL** *rises.*

TIME'S ON THE WING, MY LOVE,
AND TIME IS FLEET.

CARL *crosses to right of* **SARI**.

CARL

PEACE ENFOLD YOU,
HERE IN MY ARMS I WILL HOLD YOU;
FEARS RECEDING
FURTHER AND FURTHER AWAY.

They go slowly back to table down right.

SARI

PEACE ENFOLD ME,
HERE IN YOUR ARMS YOU WILL HOLD ME;
FEARS RECEDING
FURTHER AND FURTHER AWAY.

CARL *sits on table,* **SARI** *sits on chair left of it.*

THOUGH THE WORLD MAY DIVIDE US
AND ILL FORTUNE BETIDE US,
YET OUR LOVE IS A TOKEN
THAT CANNOT BE BROKEN
OR STOLEN AWAY.
THERE'S A PASSIONATE GLORY
IN THE HEART OF OUR STORY;
WE HAVE SOMETHING TO GUIDE US
EVERMORE AND A DAY.

SARI *crosses to centre.* **CARL** *follows to right of her.*

BOTH

THO' THE WORLD MAY DIVIDE US
AND ILL FORTUNE BETIDE US,
YET OUR LOVE IS A TOKEN
THAT CANNOT BE BROKEN

OR STOLEN AWAY.
THERE'S A PASSIONATE GLORY
IN THE HEART OF OUR STORY;
WE HAVE SOMETHING TO GUIDE US
EVERMORE AND A DAY.

SARI

EVERMORE AND A DAY.
FEARS RECEDING
FURTHER AND FURTHER AWAY.

They kiss and walk backwards and forwards across the stage as they speak the next six or seven lines, ending up at centre.

CARL We'll go away, then, tomorrow!

SARI Carl!

CARL We have a little money saved anyhow, and I hate Schlick and this place as much as you do really—tonight is the end of it—we'll go to Buda-Pesth; Fritz is there, he'll help us!

SARI Tonight is the end of it!

CARL You remember Fritz, with the long brown beard? You laughed at him.

SARI Yes, he was funny, but I liked him.

CARL Do you remember when he threw the chicken at his wife?

They both laugh.

SARI Yes! And she was so angry and the gravy ran all down the front of her.

Both laugh again.

CARL Do you feel happier now?

SARI Much, much happier.

CARL So do I! Soon we'll be able to start our own little café.

SARI That's right, let's talk about the café—where shall we have it? —how shall we manage it?

SARI goes up to table at centre below bandstand, and sits on right of it. CARL follows and sits on the table beside her on her left.

Shall I be able to sing your songs there? One day I might make them famous. I love your music so very much—I want it to be known all over the world and one day it will be, I'm sure of it!

CARL Darling!

They kiss and then, still sitting side by side on the table, start to sing.

DUET: "DEAR LITTLE CAFÉ"

SARI *and* **CARL**.

CARL

WE SHARE A MUTUAL AMBITION
WHICH NAUGHT CAN DISARRANGE,

SARI

BASED ON THE HOPEFUL SUPPOSITION
THAT SOON OUR LUCK WILL CHANGE.

They hold hands for the next two lines.

CARL

THO' WE VERY OFTEN WONDER WHETHER
POVERTY WILL WIN THE DAY,

SARI

JUST AS LONG AS WE REMAIN TOGETHER
TROUBLES SEEM TO FADE AWAY.

BOTH

HOWEVER HARD THE BED ONE LIES ON
THE SAME OLD DREAMS BEGIN,

WE'RE ALWAYS SCANNING THE HORIZON
FOR WHEN OUR SHIP COMES IN.

Refrain.

CARL

WE'LL HAVE A SWEET LITTLE CAFÉ
IN A NEAT LITTLE SQUARE,

SARI

WE'LL FIND OUR FORTUNE
AND OUR HAPPINESS THERE.

CARL

WE SHALL THRIVE ON THE VAIN AND RESPLENDENT

SARI

AND CONTRIVE TO REMAIN INDEPENDENT.

CARL

WE'LL HAVE A MEEK REPUTATION
AND A CHIC CLIENTÈLE.

SARI

KINGS WILL FALL UNDER OUR SPELL.

BOTH

WE'LL BE SO ZEALOUS
THAT THE WORLD WILL BE JEALOUS
OF OUR SWEET LITTLE CAFÉ IN OUR SQUARE.

SARI

CAN YOU IMAGINE OUR SENSATIONS
WHEN WE'VE SECURITY?

CARL

AND ALL OUR DREARY DEPRIVATIONS
ARE JUST A MEMORY?

SARI

THO' WE'RE VERY OFTEN DRIVEN FRANTIC,
PEACE IS VERY HARD TO FIND.

CARL

>ALL THESE DREADFUL DAYS WILL SEEM ROMANTIC
>WHEN WE'VE LEFT THEM FAR BEHIND.

BOTH

>FATE NEEDN'T BE QUITE SUCH A DRAGON,
>HE KNOWS HOW TIRED WE ARE.
>WE'LL HITCH OUR HOPEFUL LITTLE WAGON
>ON TO A LUCKY STAR.
>
>*Refrain.*

CARL

>WE'LL HAVE A SWEET LITTLE CAFÉ
>IN A NEAT LITTLE SQUARE,

SARI

>WE'LL FIND OUR FORTUNE
>AND OUR HAPPINESS THERE.

CARL

>WE SHALL THRIVE ON THE VAIN AND RESPLENDENT

SARI

>AND CONTRIVE TO REMAIN INDEPENDENT.

CARL

>WE'LL HAVE A MEEK REPUTATION
>AND A CHIC CLIENTÈLE.
>
>**SARI** *rises and comes down stage a little.*

SARI

>KINGS WILL FALL UNDER OUR SPELL.
>
>**CARL** *follows her.*

BOTH

>WE'LL BE SO ZEALOUS
>THAT THE WORLD WILL BE JEALOUS
>
>*Lighting – fade out everything so that there is a complete black out by the time, the last word of the number is sung.*
>
>OF OUR SWEET LITTLE CAFE IN OUR SQUARE.

They start to go out by the street door, but, being thirsty, **CARL** *whistles and a* **WAITER** *enters from up right.* **CARL** *orders drinks, the* **WAITER** *exits up right and* **CARL** *and* **SARI** *bring the centre table down stage a few paces. They then bring down the two chairs and put them right and left of the table.* **CARL** *gets the cloth from the table down left and puts it on the centre table,* **CARL** *sits left.* **SARI** *sits right. The* **WAITER** *returns with two glasses of coffee on a tray and then gets a violin and bow from the bandstand and plays while* **SARI** *and* **CARL** *sing.*

BOTH
WE'LL BE SO ZEALOUS
THAT THE WORLD WILL BE JEALOUS
OF OUR SWEET LITTLE CAFÉ IN OUR SQUARE.

Curtain down on the word "square".

Lighting – working light.

Scene Two

The Interior of **HERR SCHLICK**'s *Café in Vienna in 1880.*

The scene is the same as ACT II, Scene One, except that it is now about 2 a.m. the next morning and consequently the café is now arranged with the chairs and tables in order. The tables down right and left remain. The table down centre has been taken to the back.

Lighting – full up everything. All fittings alight.

CARL *is conducting his band. About a dozen couples are waltzing and* **WAITERS** *are taking down orders and delivering drinks. The* **LADIES OF THE TOWN** *are sitting down right and left, drinking and talking.*

The curtain rises at music cue and as it rises the orchestra fades out and leaves the music to the stage band, who carry on until the end of the waltz. The orchestra then takes on again and about a dozen officers come in from the street door and take partners from among the women. They group with them down stage and sing the opening number. They may do simple movements and regroup at the discretion of the producer as long as a general impression of gaiety and abandon is given. **HANSI**, **LOTTE**, **FREDA** *and* **GUSSI** *are seated at table down left.*

OFFICERS' *chorus.*

"LADIES OF THE TOWN"

OFFICERS
>WE WISH TO ORDER WINE, PLEASE,
EXPRESSLY FROM THE RHINE, PLEASE,
THE YEAR WE REALLY DON'T MUCH CARE.

LADIES

OH DEAR,
NOW THAT YOU'RE HERE
THINK OF THE WEAR AND TEAR.

OFFICERS

WE HOPE WITHOUT INSISTENCE
TO OVERCOME RESISTANCE
IN ALL YOU LITTLE LADIES FAIR.

LADIES

OH WELL,
HOW CAN WE TELL
WHETHER YOU'D REALLY DARE?

OFFICERS

WE SINCERELY HOPE IT'S REALLY NOT A THANKLESS TASK
AMUSING US,
WON'T YOU PLEASE AGREE?

LADIES

AH, ME!

OFFICERS

YOU COULD QUICKLY BREAK OUR HEARTS BY EVERYTHING
   WE ASK
REFUSING US;
CRUEL THAT WOULD BE,
LADIES, CAN'T YOU SEE!
WE'RE

ALL

OFFICERS AND GENTLEMEN,
RELIABLE AND TRUE,
CONSIDERATE AND CHIVALROUS
IN EVERYTHING WE DO.

THOUGH WE'RE GAY AND DRUNK A TRIFLE,
ALL OUR LAUGHTER WE SHOULD STIFLE,

LADIES

WERE THEY SUMMONED BY A BUGLE CALL.

ALL

> WE'RE AMOROUS AND PASSIONATE,
> BUT DIGNIFIED AND STERN,
> WHICH IF YOU PLAY US FALSE YOU'LL QUICKLY LEARN.
> DO NOT LET OUR PRESENCE GRIEVE YOU,
> WHEN WE'VE LOVED YOU WE SHALL LEAVE YOU,
> FOR WE'RE OFFICERS AND GENTLEMEN, THAT'S ALL!

OFFICERS

> YES, WE'RE OFFICERS AND GENTLEMEN.

LADIES

> YES.

ALL

> OFFICERS AND GENTLEMEN, THAT'S ALL.

> **LIEUTENANT TRANISCH** *enters from the street, gives his coat to a* **WAITER** *and puts his hat on the* **WAITER***'s head. The* **WAITER** *has a tray of glasses, which are taken by* **TRANISCH** *and the other officers. The other guests get glasses from the other* **WAITERS**. **TRANISCH** *comes down centre for his song. The* **OFFICERS** *and* **GUESTS** *group behind him in a large semicircle. A few are left at the tables.*

OFFICERS *(shouting)* Tokay!

"TOKAY"

LIEUTENANT TRANISCH *and* **CHORUS**.

TRANISCH

> WHEN WE'RE THOROUGHLY WINED AND DINED,
> AND THE BARRACKS ARE LEFT BEHIND,
> WE COME DOWN TO THE TOWN TO FIND
> SOME RELIEF FROM THE DAILY GRIND.
> LOVE IS KIND,
> LOVE IS BLIND.

OFFICERS

> TOKAY!

TRANISCH
>WHEN THE THOUGHTS OF A MAN INCLINE
>TO THE GRAPES OF A SUNLIT VINE,
>ON THE BANKS OF THE GOLDEN RHINE,
>SLOWLY RIPENING PURE AND FINE,
>SWEET DIVINE,
>LOVER'S WINE.
>LIFT YOUR VOICES TILL THE RAFTERS RING,
>FILL YOUR GLASSES TO THE BRIM AND SING:
>
>*Refrain.*
>
>TOKAY!
>THE GOLDEN SUNSHINE OF A SUMMER DAY,
>TOKAY!
>WILL BEAR THE BURDEN OF YOUR CARES AWAY.
>HERE'S TO THE LOVE IN YOU,
>THE HATE IN YOU,
>DESIRE IN YOU.

OFFICERS
>WINE OF THE SUN THAT WILL WAFT YOU ALONG,
>LIFTING YOU HIGH ON THE WINGS OF A SONG.

TRANISCH
>THE DREAMS IN YOU,
>THE FLAME IN YOU,
>THE FIRE IN YOU.
>TOKAY! TOKAY!

OFFICERS
>SO WHILE FORGETFULNESS WE BORROW,
>NEVER MINDING WHAT TOMORROW HAS TO SAY,

TRANISCH
>TOKAY!
>THE ONLY CALL WE ALL OBEY,
>TOKAY! TOKAY! TOKAY!

ALL
>TOKAY!
>THE GOLDEN SUNSHINE OF A SUMMER'S DAY.

TOKAY!
WILL BEAR THE BURDEN OF YOUR CARES AWAY.
HERE'S TO THE LOVE IN YOU,
THE HATE IN YOU,
DESIRE IN YOU.

BASSES

WINE OF THE SUN THAT WILL WAFT YOU ALONG,

ALL

LIFTING YOU HIGH ON THE WINGS OF A SONG.

TENORS AND BASSES

THE DREAMS IN YOU,
THE FLAME IN YOU,
THE FIRE IN YOU,

ALL

TOKAY! TOKAY!
SO WHILE FORGETFULNESS WE BORROW,
NEVER MINDING WHAT THE MORROW
HAS TO SAY.

TENORS AND BASSES

NEVER MINDING WHAT THE MORROW
HAS TO SAY.

ALL

TOKAY!
THE ONLY CALL WE ALL OBEY,
TOKAY! TOKAY! TOKAY!

Should it be considered necessary to reduce the length of the production, the dialogue from here to "...leave tomorrow without your money and be damned to you" on page 85 can be omitted.

Should the following dialogue be used, **MANON** *and* **SARI** *enter from down left and cross to table down right and sit in chairs left of table,* **SARI** *down stage.*

The **CHORUS** *disperses to various tables and sit quietly laughing, talking, ordering and drinking wine, etc.*

TRANISCH *goes out down left with* **HANSI**, **FREDA** *and* **GUSSI** *and one or two officers.*

SARI I'm so tired.

MANON Well, for heaven's sake don't look as if you were.

SARI I'm sick of pretending.

MANON So am I, but it's no use worrying about that. The whole business is pretending. Life's pretending.

SARI That hateful Captain August—he smiled at me in the bar—an odious smile.

MANON I hope you smiled back.

SARI I certainly did not.

MANON Well, that was very foolish of you—there's nothing so alluring to that type of man as snowy chastity.

SARI How can you, Manon! *(She smiles)* I'm so miserable really, it's horrid of you to laugh at me.

MANON That's better—you're smiling yourself now.

LIEUTENANT TRANISCH *enters from down left, comes to table down right and bows to* **MANON**.

TRANISCH Mademoiselle la Crevette.

MANON Yes?

TRANISCH We have never spoken before, but I wish to say you are an admirable artiste—you sing like an angel.

MANON *(laughing very loudly)* You Viennese are so gallant. I sing like a frog.

TRANISCH Will you come to the bar and take a drink with me?

MANON What is this now—what does this mean? Is it the birth of a romance? I feel so flattered.

TRANISCH *(slightly embarrassed)* Mademoiselle—I—

MANON Never mind, Lieutenant, I am not deceived—you think I sing well, that is very kind—now tell me—cards on the table—to which of the more attractive women here do you want me to introduce you?

TRANISCH Really—you misunderstand me—I—

MANON Come now—tell me—I have no sensibilites.

TRANISCH There is a small blonde lady like a kitten in yellow—I will admit to you frankly—she enthrals me strangely.

MANON That would be Gussi. *(She rises)* Excuse me for a moment, Sari.

SARI Of course.

TRANISCH *(clicking his heels and bowing to* **SARI***)* Fräulein.

MANON Come along—but let me warn you—Gussi is a collector.

TRANISCH Collector?

MANON Yes, of antiques—very enthusiastic—old jewellery for preference. If your acquaintance ripens, let me advise you when walking to keep to the more modern thoroughfares. *(She looks at* **SARI** *smilingly)* Heigh-ho—if love were all!

She and **TRANISCH** *go off down left.* **CAPTAIN AUGUST LUTTE** *enters from street door and comes to* **SARI***'s table, but as he does so* **CARL** *sees him and comes down from the bandstand.*

CAPTAIN *(on left of* **SARI***, bowing)* Madame—

CARL *(coming between them)* Sari, I want to talk to you. You remember the second movement in the concerto I was scoring yesterday, I have had the most magnificent idea—instead of using strings alone, I shall strengthen it with the zimbale just towards the end where it goes—tum tum tum tum— *(He hums)*

SARI Yes, I know—*what* a good idea! *(She also hums)* Tum tum—tum tum tum—

They both hum together, and finally **CAPTAIN AUGUST LUTTE**, *finding himself completely ignored, turns on his heel and marches off down left.*

(half laughing) Oh, Carl—that was wonderful of you.

CARL I was watching—I'm always watching to see that no harm comes to you.

SARI I hate him so—he won't leave me alone—he embarrasses me.

CARL Cheer up, my dearest.

SARI I'll try. *(She smiles)* Oh, Carl, there's something so heavy weighing down on my heart—I felt it this morning, and it's there again now.

CARL *(looking at her)* You're very strange tonight—you've been strange all day—eager and tense like a frightened child. Is there anything the matter really?

SARI Yes—no—I don't know. I feel as though fate were too strong for us, as though our love for one another and our happiness together was making the gods angry. I feel suddenly insecure.

CARL We'll go away, then, tomorrow, as we planned.

SARI Carl!

CARL I must get back. Au revoir, my dear love.

SARI Au revoir.

She kisses her hand to him and goes off up right. **CARL** *returns to band.* **GUSSI** *and* **LIEUTENANT TRANISCH** *come on from down left, followed by* **HANSI** *and* **FREDA**, *who are giggling.* **SCHLICK** *enters from up left and talks to two officers at left centre.*

GUSSI Louis Quinze—of course it was only paste, but definitely Louis Quinze.

TRANISCH How interesting!

GUSSI I'll show it to you tomorrow—we can drive there after luncheon.

TRANISCH We haven't had supper yet.

GUSSI No, but we will—we'll sit here—I shall have to dance in a minute—Fritz—Hans—

She sits down with **TRANISCH** *at table down left and calls the* **WAITERS**. **FREDA** *and* **HANSI** *cross and sit at table down right.*

HANSI I'll tell you one thing here and now, whatever Gussi is talking about is *not* paste.

FREDA I doubt if it's even Louis Quinze.

SARI comes in from up right and crosses to table down right.

HANSI Here comes the snow queen.

FREDA Hullo, Sari.

SARI Hullo *(Sits left of table)*

HANSI Any offers tonight?

FREDA Don't tease her, Hansi—she's in love.

SARI *(smiling)* No, no offers so far.

HANSI Do you want a drink?

SARI Yes—I'd love one.

HANSI Fritz—

She calls the **WAITER** *and orders wine.*

FREDA That's pretty, that dress—is it new?

SARI Yes. I made it myself from a pattern.

FREDA It sags a little bit behind—here—look—give me a pin, Hansi.

HANSI You can have this brooch for the time being, but give it back, it's not valuable, but lucky.

She gives **SARI** *a brooch,* **SARI** *stands up while* **FREDA** *fixes the brooch on to the dress.* **CAPTAIN AUGUST LUTTE** *comes in from down left, crosses right and bows ironically to* **SARI**.

CAPTAIN Will you honour me with this dance, please?

SARI (*jumping slightly*) Oh—no, I'm sorry—I'm engaged.

CAPTAIN I fear that is not strictly true.

FREDA I'll dance with you, if you like.

CAPTAIN Please do not think me impolite, but I have set my heart on dancing with Fräulein Sari.

SARI Forgive me, Captain, but it's quite impossible.

CAPTAIN We shall see.

He bows abruptly and walks across the stage to where **SCHLICK** *is standing talking to two* **OFFICERS** *at left centre. He is obviously very angry. He speaks to* **SCHLICK** *swiftly and angrily.*

SARI I hate him—he's always tormenting me.

FREDA You're unwise, my dear—it's best to humour them a little.

SARI I've tried—I've danced with him, but he presses me too close and whispers horrible things to me.

HANSI He's very rich and, I believe, generous.

SARI Yes, but that doesn't interest me.

HANSI (*wistfully*) There's no doubt about it—love is very bad for business.

ced **SCHLICK** *comes to their table.*

SCHLICK Sari—

SARI Yes, Herr Schlick.

SCHLICK You are engaged and paid by me as a dancing partner for my clients, are you not?

SARI Yes.

SCHLICK I have received several complaints from Captain August Lutte—he says you persistently refuse to dance with him.

SARI He takes advantage of my position.

SCHLICK It would be better if you realized once and for all that you have no position—after tonight you may consider your engagement at an end.

SARI *(with spirit)* It is at end anyhow—my husband and I are leaving Vienna tomorrow.

SCHLICK Oho—I see. Well, I should like to remind you that you both have a week's salary owing to you, and unless you dance willingly and agreeably with Captain August or any other of the officers when they ask you to, neither you nor your husband will receive a penny of your salary—I run my café on business lines, you understand.

SARI But, Herr Schlick, that is unfair—my behaviour has nothing to do with my husband.

SCHLICK That is enough. I am sick to death of your stupid mincing airs and graces—unless you behave yourself tonight, you will both leave tomorrow without your money, and be damned to you!

He leaves **SARI**, *who crosses to table down left and sits on right of it.* **CAPTAIN AUGUST LUTTE** *crosses right and sits in downstage chair on left of table down right.* **SCHLICK** *advances to the middle of the floor to announce the commencement of the entertainment.*

In the event of the previous dialogue being cut, as soon as the **"TOKAY"** *number is over,* **HERR SCHLICK** *enters from up left and comes to left centre.* **TRANISCH** *and two* **OFFICERS** *exit down left. The stage band strikes* *up a waltz and dancing begins.* **SARI** *enters from up right and makes her way down to centre, where she is met by the* **CAPTAIN**, *who has just come in from down left. He tries to take her hand but she brushes him aside and sits at right of table down left. The* **CAPTAIN** *turns furiously to* **SCHLICK** *who, after receiving his complaint, crosses to* **SARI** *and reprimands her in dumb show. The* **CAPTAIN** *crosses right and sits in downstage chair on left of table down right.* **SCHLICK** *goes to centre to make the following announcement and, as he does so, the band and the dancers stop.*

Ladies and Gentlemen, I crave your kind attention for the most superb musical entertainment ever offered in Vienna.

Everyone applauds.

Thank you. Thank you. My first number will be my six magnificent dancing girls—trained exclusively in the finest ballet schools in the world. Lise, Trude, Fritz, Toni, Greta and Elsa, the Prater Girls.

The six **PRATER GIRLS** *enter from up right. Three are dressed as peasant girls and three as peasant boys. They dance in single file round the bandstand and* **SCHLICK** *dances after them.* **CARL** *and his men play for them. Having made a complete circle, they form two lines across the stage down centre and do a fast jig which finishes with the three boys in front doing the splits and the three girls standing behind doing arabesques. The crowd applaud and the girls run off up left. During their dance* **SCHLICK** *stands up right centre. During the applause* **TRANISCH** *and two* **OFFICERS** *enter from down left, cross and sit upstage of the* **CAPTAIN** *at table down right.*

When the girls have gone off **SCHLICK** *again goes centre for his next announcement.*

Gentlemen—Ladies and Gentlemen—I beg attention for my favourite, your favourite, the world's favourite star—Manon la Crevette.

SCHLICK *goes back up right centre.* **MANON** *comes running up from left. She is greeted with vociferous applause as she reaches centre.*

MANON Mesdames, Messieurs, je vais vous chanter une petite chanson de ma jeunesse—a very long time ago!

She sings **"BONNE NUIT, MERCI!"** *interspersed with a good deal of back-chat and ogling. The stage band plays.*

"BONNE NUIT, MERCI!"

MANON
LORSQUE ÉTAIS PETITE FILLE
EN MARCHANT PARMI LES PRÉS
J'ENTENDIS LA VOIX D'MA TANTE
QUI MURMURAIT À CÔTÉ,
"N'OUBLIE PAS LA POLITESSE
LORSQUE VIENDRA UN AMANT
CAR TOUT LE BONHEUR RÉSIDE LÀ DEDANS."

Refrain.
C'EST POURQUOI DANS MES AFFAIRES,
SOIT DE COEUR OU SOIT D'ESPRIT,
C'EST POURQUOI JE TÂCHE DE PLAIRE
TOUTE LA FOULE DE MES AMIS,
SOIT QU'ILS M'OFFRENT PIED-À-TERRE
OU ME MONTRENT UNE BONNE AFFAIRE
J'LEUR RÉPONDS, "VAS-Y. BONNE NUIT, MERCI!"

The **CROWD** *laugh and applaud.*

MANON *(shouts)* O-oh! La, la! Je n'ai pas fini!
LORSQUE JE SUIS V'NUE À PARIS
J'ÉTAIS SAGE DE NATURE,
MAIS QUE FAIRE DANS LA VIE

ÉTANT JEUNE POUR RESTER PURE!
QUAND MA POLITESSE M'OBLIGEA
LORSQU' JE SUIVAIS PAR HASARD
UNE AVENTURE DANS LES BOÎTES DES BOULEVARDS.

Refrain.
ET J'AI RENCONTRÉ EN VILLE
UN MONSIEUR BIEN COMME IL FAUT,
IL M'A DIT, "MA PETITE FILLE,
VEUX-TU FAIRE UN P'TIT DODO?"
LORSQU' J'ARRIVE CHEZ LUI TOUT DE SUITE
I'ME DIT "DÉSHABILLE-TOI VITE!"
J'ME SUIS DIT "VAS'Y. BONNE NUIT, MERCI!"

CROWD *laugh and applaud.*

MANON *(speaking)* Mesdames, Messieurs, pour ma deuxième chanson, je chanterai une petite chanson un petit peu triste.

CROWD *sigh "Oh!".*

Just a little more sad!

CROWD *sigh "Oh!" again.*

A song of the Broken Heart!

The **CROWD** *roar with laughter,* **MANON** *points to the* **CAPTAIN.**

Il sait ce que c'est le Broken Heart, le capitaine!

The **CAPTAIN** *and the crowd roar at this,* **MANON** *takes a chair from the table down left, puts it centre and then, accompanied by the stage band, sings her next song.*

"WALTZ SONG"

MANON *and* **CHORUS.**

MANON
'TIS TIME THAT WE WERE PARTED,

Sits on her chair comically.

YOU AND I,
HOWEVER BROKEN-HEARTED,
'TIS GOOD-BYE!
ALTHOUGH OUR LOVE HAS ENDED
AND DARKNESS HAS DESCENDED,

Rises and takes the chair to left of the **CAPTAIN**, *where she sits.*

I CALL TO YOU WITH ONE LAST CRY:

Refrain.

This is deliberately sung at the **CAPTAIN**.

KISS ME
BEFORE YOU GO AWAY!
MISS ME
THROUGH EVERY NIGHT AND DAY.
THOUGH CLOUDS ARE GREY ABOVE YOU,
YOU'LL HEAR ME SAY I LOVE YOU!
KISS ME
BEFORE YOU GO AWAY!

She rises and goes centre and sings the next verse to the crowd.

PARMI LES CHANSONS TRISTES
DE L'AMOUR,
JOIES ET CHAGRINS EXISTENT
TOUR À TOUR,
ET PRESQU'AVEC CONTRAINTE
ON RISQUE LA DOUCE ÉTREINTE
QUI NOUS SÉPARE ENFIN TOUJOURS.

She goes right again to the **CAPTAIN** *and teases him with the next refrain. The* **CHORUS** *can join in as much as they like.*

Refrain.

JE T'AIME,
TES BAISERS M'ONT GRISÉS
MÊME
À L'HEURE DE T'EN ALLER,
LA VOLUPTÉ TROUBLANTE
BRISE MES LÈVRES BRÛLANTES,
JE T'AIME,
À L'HEURE DE T'EN ALLER.

At the end she skips off up left as the crowd applaud. She takes three calls and the stage band give her a chord for each bow.

At the end of this **CARL** *strikes up another waltz and everybody begins to dance,* **SCHLICK** *comes over to* **SARI***'s table. After a moment the* **CAPTAIN** *approaches and bows.*

The following few lines are not heard through the noise of the dance and are more pantomimed than spoken.

CAPTAIN Fräulein Sari has perhaps by now forgotten her other engagement.

SARI *(rising agitatedly)* I—please—I—

SCHLICK You are quite right, Captain, she has forgotten.

SARI Captain August—I am very tired—will you please forgive me just this once?

CAPTAIN One dance, please.

SCHLICK I think you would be well advised to grant Captain August's request.

SARI *(pulling herself together)* Certainly, Captain, I shall be charmed.

She gives one despairing look at **CARL** *on the dais— he is watching anxiously—then she surrenders herself to the* **CAPTAIN***'s arms and they begin to waltz,* **CARL** *watches all the time. As the dance progresses the* **CAPTAIN** *is obviously becoming more and more aggressively amorous.* **CARL,** *with obvious agitation, perceptibly quickens the tempo of the music. Finally the* **CAPTAIN** *waltzes* **SARI** *into the centre of the floor—stops dead, tightens his arms round her and kisses her on the mouth passionately, bending her right back as he does so. She gives one cry,* **CARL** *stops the music dead with a crash and leaps over the railing of the dais on to the middle of the floor. He drags* **SARI** *away from the* **CAPTAIN,** *then, springing at him, strikes him in the face. Everyone springs up. Immediately the buzz of excitement dies down into dead silence.*

MANON *enters from up left and comes quickly down to left of* **SARI,** *who is up centre.*

CARL *(wildly)* Swine—filthy, ill-mannered drunken swine!

SARI *(in a whisper)* Carl!

MANON *(rushing forward)* Carl—don't be a fool.

The **CAPTAIN** *gives an unpleasant laugh.*

CAPTAIN Tranisch—look after our foolhardy young friend here, will you?

TRANISCH Not now—not now—wait.

CAPTAIN I regret—I cannot wait.

TRANISCH *crosses quickly to the wall behind the table down left and takes two of the swords hanging there. He gives one to* **CARL** *and keeps one himself. One of the other* **OFFICERS** *on the left takes the third sword and hands it to the* **CAPTAIN,** *who goes to right centre and faces* **CARL** *at left centre.* **TRANISCH** *stands at centre up stage of them to act as umpire.* **SARI** *is on the left of* **TRANISCH,** *slightly up stage of him.* **SCHLICK** *is up left centre. The* **CROWD** *stand round in a semicircle.*

CARL Stand back, Manon—look after Sari—please.

> TRANISCH *holds his sword under the swords of* CARL *and the* CAPTAIN. *As he says "On guard" he strikes their swords upwards and steps back, leaving them to fight.*

TRANISCH On guard!

> *The* CAPTAIN *and* CARL *fight a brief duel. Suddenly the* CAPTAIN *knocks* CARL's *sword from his hand and runs him through.*

> *Note – The actual fencing must depend on the capabilities of the two actors, but it should be made obvious that the* CAPTAIN *is merely playing with* CARL, *and it is effective if he knocks* CARL's *sword out of his hand twice. The first time it is returned to* CARL *by one of the* OFFICERS *on the left, the* CAPTAIN *standing to attention meanwhile.*

> *There is a general scream and everyone crowds forward,* SARI *silently sinks to the ground, taking* CARL *in her arms. There is silence.*

SARI *(softly—she is dry-eyed)* I'll love you always—always—do you hear?

CARL *(weakly)* Sari—Sari—my sweet, sweet Sari—

> *His head falls back in her lap, and she kneels there staring before her dazed and hopeless. The absolute silence is only broken after* CARL *dies, and then only by the sobbing of* MANON.

> *The* CAPTAIN *salutes.*

> *The curtain is lowered slowly as* CARL's *head falls back.*

> *Lighting – front-of-house arcs and floats out.*

Second Interval

ACT III

Scene One

*The **MARQUIS OF SHAYNE**'s house in Grosvenor Square in 1895.*

It is the same room that was used for ACT I, Scene One. The decorations and most of the furniture have been changed. There is a grand piano and stool up centre and chairs and settees round the sides. The entrances are the same as ACT I, Scene One.

Lighting – full up everything.

*The curtain rises at music cue and during the ensuing music the **GUESTS** come in through the door up right. The **BUTLER** announces them and **LORD SHAYNE** stands just inside to receive them. Several guests are already in the room, grouped and talking. Among them are **MR** and **MRS VALE** (**JANE**) and **MR** and **MRS BETHEL** (**EFFIE**). The names are announced in the following order by the **BUTLER**:*

1. Mr and Mrs Arthur Meadows.

2. Mr and Mrs Proutie (Gloria).

3. Mr and Mrs Titian Naylor.

4. Miss Mosscrock.

5. The Duke and Duchess of Tenterden (Victoria)

6. Sir George and Lady Churt.

7. Lord and Lady Sorrel (Honor).

8. Lord and Lady Edgar James (Harriet).

When everyone is on stage, the **BUTLER** *exits and shuts the door up right. The six couples (***VALES**, **PROUTIES**, **BETHELS**, **TENTERDENS**, **SORRELS** *and* **JAMES***) come down line in front centre with each husband slightly behind his wife. They sing the opening chorus while the others sit and group round the room.*

Opening chorus.

Double Sextette.

ALL
>TARARA BOOM-DE-AY,
>TARARA BOOM-DE-AY,
>WE ARE THE MOST EFFECTUAL,
>INTELLECTUAL
>MOVEMENT OF THE DAY.
>OUR MORAL STANDARDS SWAY
>LIKE MRS TANQUERAY
>AND WE ARE THEORETICALLY
>MOST AESTHETICALLY
>EAGER TO DISPLAY
>THE FACT THAT WE'RE AGGRESSIVELY
>AND EXCESSIVELY
>ANXIOUS TO DESTROY
>ALL THE SNOBBERY
>AND HOB-NOBBERY
>OF THE HOI-POLLOI.
>TARARA BOOM-DE-AY.
>IT'S MENTAL WASHING DAY,
>AND COME WHAT MAY
>WE'LL SCRUB UNTIL THE NATION'S MORALS SHRINK AWAY.
>TARARA BOOM-DE-AY!

While the **MEN** *sing the next few lines, the* **GIRLS** *get behind them and form an oblique line on left.*

MEN

>THOUGH WE ARE LANGUID IN APPEARANCE,
>WE'RE IN THE VANGUARD.
>WE FEEL WE CAN GUARD
>THE CAUSE OF ART.
>WE SHALL IGNORE ALL INTERFERENCE,
>FOR OUR COMPLACENCE
>WITH THIS RENAISSANCE
>IS FRIGHTFULLY SMART.
>
>*The* **GIRLS** *march down left and then across the stage in front of the* **MEN** *so that each wife comes next to her husband. They sing as they march.*

GIRLS

>PLEASE DO NOT THINK US UNRELENTING,
>OUR CHARMING FROLIC
>WITH THE SYMBOLIC
>IS MEEK AND MILD.

ALL

>WE MERELY SPEND OUR TIME PREVENTING
>SOME EARNEST STRIPLING
>FROM LIKING KIPLING
>INSTEAD OF WILDE.
>NOW THAT WE FIND THE DREARY NINETEENTH CENTURY IS CLOSING,
>WE MEAN TO START THE TWENTIETH IN ECSTASIES OF POSING.

ALL

>TARARA BOOM-DE-AY,
>IT'S MENTAL WASHING DAY,
>AND COME WHAT MAY
>WE'LL SCRUB UNTIL THE TIRESOME BOURGEOIS SHRINK AWAY.
>TARARA BOOM-DE-AY!
>
>*The* **GIRLS** *take their husbands' arms, go up stage and group as the* **BUTLER** *opens the doors up left and*

announces "Refreshments are served". They then send their husbands along to supper with all the other guests, leaving only the six of them on the stage. They are arranged in a rough semicircle at c. and stand from right to left as follows: **VICTORIA, JANE, HONOR, GLORIA, EFFIE** *and* **HARRIET.** *The* **BUTLER** *closes the door up left.*

HARRIET What have you done with your hair, Effie? It strikes me as peculiar.

EFFIE *(feeling her hair)* Nothing in particular.

GLORIA I'm afraid you are becoming a little pernickety, Harriet; you must guard against it.

HONOR How's your late husband, Gloria?

GLORIA He was later than ever this evening, my dear. He was at Boodle's, I expect.

JANE Talking too much.

HARRIET And drinking too much. *(Goes up to left end of settee up right and sits)*

GLORIA *(crossing to settee and sitting upstage of* **HARRIET***)* You can't upset me by saying that, Harriet dear. I find alcohol one of the greatest comforts of matrimony.

HONOR Gloria!

GLORIA In a husband, I mean. It leaves one free for one's charities.

JANE *(crossing to behind settee up right, where she stands)* A little too free sometimes, my pet.

GLORIA You're getting old, Jane, and a trifle embittered; it's very sad.

HARRIET We're all getting old and I for one am not enjoying it.

EFFIE Age has its compensations. *(Goes up and sits on right end of settee)* We have our husbands.

JANE And our children.

GLORIA Oh dear! I wish we hadn't.

> **HONOR** *and* **VICTORIA** *remain standing up centre while the others are sitting on the settee up right (***JANE** *behind) and they all sing the next number.*

"ALAS, THE TIME IS PAST"

VICTORIA
HARRIET } ALAS, THE TIME
EFFIE

ALL
> IS PAST WHEN WE
> COULD FROLIC WITH IMPUNITY.
> SECURE IN OUR VIRGINITY,
> WE SOMETIMES LOOK AGHAST
> ADOWN THE LANES OF MEMORY,
> ALAS, THE TIME IS PAST.

VICTORIA } AH, THEN THE WORLD WAS AT OUR FEET,
GLORIA } WHEN WE WERE SWEET-AND-TWENTY,

VICTORIA
EFFIE } WE NEVER GUESSED THAT WHAT WE'D GOT,
GLORIA

ALL
> THO' NOT A LOT—WAS PLENTY.

EFFIE
> WE GAILY SOUGHT SOME ABELARD
> TO CHERISH, GUARD AND OWN US,

VICTORIA
> BUT ALL WE KNOW OF STORM AND STRIFE
> OUR MARRIED LIFE—HAS SHOWN US.

VICTORIA
HARRIET } ALAS, THE TIME
EFFIE

ALL
　IS PAST WHEN WE
　COULD FROLIC WITH IMPUNITY.
　SECURE IN OUR VIRGINITY,
　WE SOMETIMES LOOK AGHAST
　ADOWN THE LANES OF MEMORY.
　ALAS, THE TIME IS PAST.

GLORIA
　ALACK-A-DAY ME—

EFFIE
　ALACK-A-DAY ME!

ALL
　ALACK-A-DAY ME! AH, THEN THE WORLD WAS AT OUR FEET,
　ALAS, THE TIME IS PAST.

HARRIET Who is this woman?

EFFIE Which woman?

HARRIET The one we've been invited to meet.

VICTORIA Some strange Hungarian singer—probably very glittering and rather stout.

HONOR *(going down a little right)* Oh, I shouldn't think so—Lord Shayne has been pursuing her for ages from capital to capital.

HARRIET Central Europe is far too musical, there can be no two opinions about that.

JANE I hear she's very beautiful.

　LORD SHAYNE *has entered unobserved from up left. He comes down between* **VICTORIA** *and the settee.*

LORD SHAYNE She is—

VICTORIA Good heavens, how you made me jump!

LORD SHAYNE She is one of the few really beautiful people in the world.

HARRIET How very disconcerting!

HONOR Do you think we shall like that?

LORD SHAYNE I shall be very interested to see the effect she has on you—you are all—if I may say so—so very representative.

VICTORIA Of what, dear Lord Shayne?

LORD SHAYNE Shall we say "fin de siècle"?

HARRIET I was afraid somebody would say that before the evening was over.

> *The* **BUTLER** *opens the door up right and announces the* **HON. HUGH DEVON** *and* **MRS DEVON**. **LORD SHAYNE** *moves over to greet them. The* **BUTLER** *closes the door.* **HUGH** *has developed along the exact lines that one would have expected; he has become a good deal more pompous with the years, and has a tremendously diplomatic manner. His wife is fat and vague. The* **GIRLS** *on settee rise and group upstage.*

VICTORIA *(coming down stage and meeting* **MRS DEVON** *at centre)* Margaret dear, how are you?

MRS. DEVON Shattered, completely shattered! Our cabby was raving mad. He kept saying the oddest things to his horse, at least I hope they were to his horse.

> **HUGH** *and* **LORD SHAYNE** *come down right.*

LORD SHAYNE I hear you're going to Vienna.

HUGH Yes, next week, thank God! I believe Mullins has been making a fearful hash of everything.

MRS. DEVON *(turning to* **LORD SHAYNE***)* Isn't it exciting! I was so afraid we were going to be sent to Riga or Christiania or somewhere draughty like that.

HARRIET *(crosses to right of piano)* Hugh generally gets what he wants.

MRS. DEVON As it is, I don't know what I shall do with the children. I can't help feeling that Eva is the wrong age for Vienna.

LORD SHAYNE No one is the wrong age for Vienna—it's a city of enchantment—magnificent.

HUGH I'm told the plumbing is appalling.

VICTORIA Lord Shayne has fallen in love again—haven't you, my dear?

LORD SHAYNE I am always in love with beauty.

VICTORIA goes up to HARRIET by the piano.

HUGH Admirably put, Shayne. I quite agree with you.

JANE *(coming down stage to HUGH)* We're all on tenterhooks to see Madame Linden—she's due at any moment.

MRS. DEVON *(crossing to mirror down left)* What are tenterhooks? I never know.

The BUTLER throws open the doors up right and announces MADAME SARI LINDEN. The girls group at left centre and watch the door. SARI enters, exquisitely gowned and radiantly beautiful, carrying herself with tremendous poise; her jewels are superb, and the years have invested her with a certain air of decision which is almost metallic as compared with the tremulous diffidence of her youth. The BUTLER closes the door. LORD SHAYNE goes forward and kisses her hand. They meet up centre.

LORD SHAYNE My dear, how enchanting to see you again! *(He turns with a smile)* I think you know everyone here.

HARRIET Good heavens, Sarah!

VICTORIA *(astounded)* Sarah!

EFFIE It can't be—it can't be—

She rushes up and kisses her. There is a babel of surprised and excited conversation. HUGH *stands down right, looking a trifle embarrassed.*

The GIRLS *crowd round* SARI *and bring her down stage centre.* MRS DEVON *walks round the back of them and comes down to* HUGH *on right.*

LORD SHAYNE *stands by the piano looking on.*

HONOR We heard that you had died, ages and ages ago.

SARI I did die. Fifteen years ago to be exact. Things happened and I couldn't come back. I didn't want to come back, so I thought I'd better die, vaguely and obscurely. It was the only thing to do—it sort of rounded everything off so satisfactorily.

JANE It's unbelievable, Sarah, dear Sarah.

SARI Please don't be quite so pleased to see me. It makes me feel ashamed, particularly with Hugh standing there, looking so stern. How do you do, Hugh?

She crosses to him and they shake hands, formally, HONOR, GLORIA *and* JANE *go up stage to* LORD SHAYNE. VICTORIA, HARRIET *and* EFFIE *group at left centre.*

HUGH I'm delighted to see you again. Margaret, I want you to meet Sarah—Sarah—? *(He looks questioningly at her)*

SARI Linden—don't say you've forgotten Carl Linden, the man I eloped with, practically under your nose, Hugh?

HUGH I remember perfectly—how is he?

SARI He's dead—I'm so glad to meet you, Mrs Devon. I do hope Hugh is a charming husband and not too embittered—I treated him abominably, you know.

MRS. DEVON *(shaking hands with her)* It's all so very surprising—very, very surprising—Hugh told me the whole story, when he heard of your death in Prague or somewhere. He was dreadfully upset, weren't you, Hugh?

HUGH Yes, indeed, I was.

SARI *(smiling and tapping him lightly with her fan)* Dear Hugh, never mind—everything always turns out for the best, doesn't it? At least, almost everything.

The **BUTLER** *opens the door up left.* **SARI** *turns centre.* **LORD SHAYNE** *comes down to her.*

LORD SHAYNE Won't you have a little supper—Sari?

HONOR "Sari"—it does sound pretty, doesn't it?

SARI Only a very little, if you want me to sing for you. *(To* **GIRLS***)* Come along, all my bridesmaids that nearly were.

They all go out up left laughing and talking. **HUGH** *and* **MRS DEVON** *are last. As they go up to the door,* **MRS DEVON** *speaks.*

MRS DEVON Very pretty, my dear, but passé, distinctly passé.

HUGH *and* **MRS DEVON** *exit after the others. When the supper-room doors close behind them, doors up right open and four over-exquisitely dressed* **YOUNG MEN** *enter. They all wear in their immaculate buttonholes green carnations.* **VERNON CRAFT,** *a poet,* **CEDRIC BALANTYNE,** *a painter,* **LORD HENRY JADE,** *a dilettante, and* **BERTRAM SELLICK,** *a playwright.*

VERNON *comes down right.* **CEDRIC** *stays up right.* **HENRY** *comes down left.* **BERTRAM** *crosses up left. All pose affectedly.*

BERTRAM It's entirely Vernon's fault that we are so entrancingly late.

VERNON My silk socks were two poems this evening and they refused to scan.

HENRY It's going to be inexpressibly dreary, I can feel it in my bones.

CEDRIC Don't be absurd, Henry, your whole charm lies in the fact that you have no bones.

All come down centre. and form a line across the stage.

QUARTETTE: "WE ALL WORE A GREEN CARNATION"

VERNON, CEDRIC, HENRY, BERTRAM.

BLASÉ BOYS ARE WE,
EXQUISITELY FREE
FROM THE DREARY AND QUITE ABSURD
MORAL VIEWS OF THE COMMON HERD.
WE LIKE PORPHYRY BOWLS,
CHANDELIERS AND STOLES,
WE'RE MOST SPIRITED,
CAREFULLY FILLETED "SOULS".

1st refrain.

PRETTY BOYS, WITTY BOYS, TOO, TOO, TOO
LAZY TO FIGHT STAGNATION,
HAUGHTY BOYS, NAUGHTY BOYS, ALL WE DO
IS TO PURSUE SENSATION.
THE PORTALS OF SOCIETY
ARE ALWAYS OPENED WIDE,
THE WORLD OUR ECCENTRICITY CONDONES,
A NOTE OF QUAINT VARIETY
WE'RE CERTAIN TO PROVIDE.
WE DRESS IN VERY DECORATIVE TONES.
FADED BOYS, JADED BOYS, WOMANKIND'S
GIFT TO A BULLDOG NATION,
IN ORDER TO DISTINGUISH US FROM LESS ENLIGHTENED MINDS,
WE ALL WEAR A GREEN CARNATION.

All move slowly to right centre and stand with their hands on each other's shoulders.

WE BELIEVE IN ART,
THOUGH WE'RE POLES APART
FROM THE FOOLS WHO ARE THRILLED BY GREUZE.
WE LIKE BEARDSLEY AND GREEN CHARTREUSE.
WOMEN SAY WE'RE TOO
BORED TO BILL AND COO,
WE SMILE WEARILY,
IT'S SO DREARILY TRUE!

All drop their hands and go back to centre.

2nd refrain.

PRETTY BOYS, WITTY BOYS, YOU MAY SNEER
AT OUR DISINTEGRATION,
HAUGHTY BOYS, NAUGHTY BOYS, DEAR, DEAR, DEAR!
SWOONING WITH AFFECTATION.
OUR FIGURES SLEEK AND WILLOWY,
OUR LIPS INCARNADINE,
MAY WORRY THE MAJORITY A BIT.
BUT MATRONS RICH AND BILLOWY
INVITE US OUT TO DINE,
AND REVEL IN OUR PHOSPHORESCENT WIT.

All move up stage into a group by settee up left centre.

FADED BOYS, JADED BOYS, COME WHAT MAY,
ART IS OUR INSPIRATION,
AND AS WE ARE THE REASON FOR THE "NINETIES" BEING GAY,
WE ALL WEAR A GREEN CARNATION.

All pose in extravagant attitudes—one sitting on the settee. As the music starts for the next refrain, they all come down front to their original positions.

3rd refrain.

PRETTY BOYS, WITTY BOYS, YEARNING FOR
PERMANENT ADULATION,
HAUGHTY BOYS, NAUGHTY BOYS, EVERY PORE
BURSTING WITH SELF-INFLATION,
WE FEEL WE'RE RATHER GRECIAN,

All take Greek poses.

AS OUR MANNERS INDICATE,
OUR SENSE OF MORAL VALUES ISN'T STRONG.
FOR ULTIMATE COMPLETION
WE SHALL REALLY HAVE TO WAIT
UNTIL THE DAY OF JUDGMENT COMES ALONG.

All go up stage in line with the exit down left.

FADED BOYS, JADED BOYS, EACH ONE CRAVES
SOME SORT OF SOUL SALVATION,
BUT WHEN WE RISE RELUCTANTLY BUT GRACEFULLY FROM OUR GRAVES,

Instead of singing the last line they march off in time with the orchestra which plays it.

LORD SHAYNE *and* **SARI** *come in from up left and cross to the piano.*

LORD SHAYNE And my dear, you will sing for us, won't you?

SARI Has your piano been tuned for me. I don't trust English pianos! *(She plays a chord or two)*

LORD SHAYNE I want to talk to you.

SARI I know. *(She sits and starts to improvise softly)*

LORD SHAYNE You can guess what I am going to say?

SARI Yes, I think so.

LORD SHAYNE I love you.

SARI *(smiling)* I was right.

LORD SHAYNE Will you honour me by becoming my wife? *(He turns front)* You've now refused me in practically every capital in Europe—London is the last on the list.

SARI Why should London prove the exception?

LORD SHAYNE It's home.

SARI *(sighing)* Yes—I suppose it is.

LORD SHAYNE It has charm, London—a very peaceful charm, particularly for anyone who is tired like you. You can drive in the Park in the spring and look at the crocuses.

SARI Please don't talk of spring.

LORD SHAYNE Then there's the autumn, when the leaves fall in the Square, and you can sit on a rickety iron chair and watch the children picking up horse chestnuts.

SARI *(stops improvising and speaks wistfully)* Whose children?

LORD SHAYNE Just anybody's.

SARI The fogs in November. *(She starts improvising again)*

LORD SHAYNE Fogs can be delightful.

SARI Can they? *(She smiles)*

LORD SHAYNE Particularly when you're warm and snug by a crackly fire, drinking tea, while from the yellow gloom outside the trees look in at you like ghosts.

SARI stops playing with a sharp discord, rises and goes down right centre.

SARI I don't like tea or ghosts.

LORD SHAYNE You're very hard to please.

SARI How do you know I'm tired?

LORD SHAYNE *(coming down on left of her)* By your voice, and your eyes.

SARI I'm afraid I don't love you—actually! I think you're kind and understanding and gay and very dear, but you know I've only really loved one man all my life. I know it's tiresome to be so faithful, particularly to a mere memory, but there it is.

LORD SHAYNE I think perhaps I could make you happy—anyhow happier.

SARI May I think it over a little? I'll let you know a little later—definitely. *(Turns and goes up centre)*

ACT III, SCENE ONE

Up left the supper-room doors are opened, by the BUTLER *and everyone comes noisily into the room.* HONOR *and* VICTORIA *go straight to* SARI *at centre.* LORD SHAYNE *crosses over left to speak to some of the* GUESTS, SARI's *accompanist has entered with the others and stands among the people near the piano.*

VICTORIA Sarah—aren't you going to sing soon?

HONOR Do you remember our singing lessons at Madame Claire's before you met Carl Linden—I mean—Oh dear—

SARI *(smiling)* I remember! I do hope my voice has improved since then.

LORD SHAYNE *(moving to left centre)* Silence, please! Madame Sari Linden will sing us some of Carl Linden's enchanting songs, the songs she has made so famous.

All applaud and arrange themselves round the room. The BUTLER *shuts the door.*

SARI *(going up to piano)* Where is my accompanist? Is he here?

The ACCOMPANIST *detaches himself from the crowd.*

LORD SHAYNE *goes up to the piano and superintends. When the pianist is seated he stands up right centre.*

ACCOMPANIST Here I am.

SARI What shall we start with?

ACCOMPANIST "The River Song"?

SARI No, that's too difficult to begin with.

ACCOMPANIST "Zigeuner"?

SARI That will do. *(Standing up centre, facing front)* Ladies and Gentlemen, this song needs a slight preface. My husband wrote it when he was only sixteen. He visited Germany for the first time and sailed down the Rhine past forests and castles and gipsy encampments, and they fired his imagination so much that he wrote this song of a lovely flaxen-haired German Princess who fell in love with a Zigeuner.

Several of the guests do not understand what a **"ZIGEUNER"** *is, so* **SARI** *explains that it means a "Gipsy".*

The **ACCOMPANIST** *starts the introduction,* **LORD SHAYNE** *stands gazing at her. She sings* **"ZIGEUNER"**.

SONG: "ZIGEUNER"

SARI.

ONCE UPON A TIME
MANY YEARS AGO,
LIVED A FAIR PRINCESS,
HATING TO CONFESS
LONELINESS WAS TORTURING HER SO.
THEN A GIPSY CAME,
CALLED TO HER BY NAME.
WOO'D HER WITH A SONG,
SENSUOUS AND STRONG,
ALL THE SUMMER LONG;
HER PASSION SEEMED TO TREMBLE LIKE A LIVING FLAME.

She comes down centre a little.

BID MY WEEPING CEASE,
MELODY THAT BRINGS
MERCIFUL RELEASE,
PROMISES OF PEACE;
THROUGH THE GENTLE THROBBINGS OF THE STRINGS.
MUSIC OF THE PLAIN,
MUSIC OF THE WILD,
COME TO ME AGAIN,
HEAR ME NOT IN VAIN,
SOOTHE A HEART IN PAIN,
AND LET ME TO MY HAPPINESS BE RECONCILED.

Refrain.

PLAY TO ME BENEATH THE SUMMER MOON,
ZIGEUNER! —ZIGEUNER! —ZIGEUNER!
ALL I ASK OF LIFE IS JUST TO LISTEN
TO THE SONGS THAT YOU SING,
MY SPIRIT LIKE A BIRD ON THE WING
YOUR MELODIES ADORING—SOARING,
CALL TO ME WITH SOME BARBARIC TUNE,
ZIGEUNER!—ZIGEUNER!—ZIGEUNER!
NOW YOU HOLD ME IN YOUR POWER,
PLAY TO ME FOR JUST AN HOUR,
ZIGEUNER!

At the end of it everyone applauds. She silences them by raising her hand. The pianist starts another tune, but **SARI** *goes up and stops him and tells him to play* ***"I'LL SEE YOU AGAIN"***.

This is a very simple, sentimental little song. I do hope you won't laugh at it—it means a very great deal to me.

She unpins a bunch of white violets from her waist and throws them to **LORD SHAYNE**. *Then she begins to sing the refrain of* ***"I'LL SEE YOU AGAIN"***.

Reprise.

I'LL SEE YOU AGAIN,
I LIVE EACH MOMENT THROUGH AGAIN.
TIME HAS LAIN HEAVY BETWEEN,
BUT WHAT HAS BEEN
CAN LEAVE ME NEVER;

She comes down centre a little.

YOUR SWEET MEMORY
ACROSS THE YEARS HAS GUIDED ME.
THOUGH MY WORLD HAS GONE AWRY,

Lighting – Fade out everything, the last to go being spot on **SARI**.

THOUGH THE YEARS MY TEARS MAY DRY,
I SHALL LOVE YOU TILL I DIE,
GOODBYE!

The curtain is lowered on the last word of the song.

Lighting – working light.

During the change **CARL**'s *voice is heard singing in the darkness.*

CARL
IF YOU WOULD ONLY COME WITH ME,
IF YOU WOULD ONLY COME WITH ME,
I'LL SEE YOU AGAIN.

Scene Two

 LADY SHAYNE's *house in Grosvenor Square at the present day.*

 The scene is exactly the same as the end of ACT I, Scene One, with everyone in the same positions.

 Lighting – fade up everything slowly to ACT I, Scene One, lighting.

 The doors up left are shut, so there is no need to change the backing. The furniture and movable panels in the walls, the ornaments and the piano are changed as quickly as possible. Quick-change rooms should be provided for the artists.

 The curtain goes up to music cue and **LADY SHAYNE** *is again an old woman singing to a lot of young people sprawling on the floor.*

SARAH Goodbye! Goodbye!

 When she finishes singing, **DOLLY CHAMBERLAIN** *springs to her feet.*

DOLLY It is the most thrilling, divine, marvellous thing I've ever heard—Vincent, I'm mad about you—d'you hear?—I love you.

 She flings herself into his arms, he gently and rather absently disengages himself.

VINCENT What a melody—my God, what a melody!

 He begins to play **"I'LL SEE YOU AGAIN"**, *softly as a foxtrot. The orchestra joins in. Everyone gets up "hey-heying" and Charlestoning and finally they all, except* **LADY SHAYNE**, **DOLLY** *and* **VINCENT**, *go jazzing out through the double doors, up right.*

LADY SHAYNE is looking at DOLLY, who is gazing adoringly at VINCENT. When he finishes playing, DOLLY makes a movement towards him.

DOLLY Vincent!

VINCENT Boys! I've got a swell tune. Listen! —Boys!

He rushes through the window as though calling to his band. DOLLY stands at left end of the piano looking stunned, LADY SHAYNE goes to her, pats her gently on the shoulder, then turns away and, moving slowly over to left, sings.

LADY SHAYNE
I SHALL LOVE YOU TILL I DIE,
GOODBYE.

She exits through door down left and as she does so the curtain descends on DOLLY standing motionless by the piano.

Lighting – front of house arcs out.

For calls—everything full up.

1st call: **LADY SHAYNE**.

2nd call: **MANON**.

3rd call: **CARL**.

4th call: Full Company.

Succeeding calls—Full company.

END

WIG AND COSTUME PLOT
ACT I
Scene One
Lady Shayne's *house. Present day.*

Lady Shayne (Sarah)—Black georgette dress with long black lace sleeves. Black satin shoes and black silk stockings. Black velvet neckband. Lorgnette. Ebony stick. Diamanté earrings. Grey wig, almost white.

Dolly Chamberlain—White satin evening dress and satin shoes to match.

Nita—Pale blue satin evening dress and satin shoes to match.

Helen—Royal blue georgette evening dress and satin shoes to match.

Lady Guests—Various evening dresses and shoes to match. Colours suggested are turquoise, rose, apple green, jade green, peach, primrose and white.

Lord Henry Jekyll / **Gentlemen Guests**—Full evening dress with white waistcoats.

Parker (Butler)—Full evening dress with black tie and waistcoat.

Vincent Howard / **Musicians**—Dinner-jackets, black waistcoats and ties.

Scene Two
The **Millicks**' *house. 1875.*

Sarah—White spotted muslin period dress with high neck and long sleeves, trimmed with frills round skirt. White frilled apron. Light peacock blue satin bow at neck, sash and buttons. White silk stockings and white satin slippers. Period wig, to suit colour of player.

Mrs. Millick—Blue velvet and silk period street dress trimmed with lace and frill at neck. Blue velvet hat trimmed with ribbon and cluster of pink roses. White gloves. Ermine muff. Black button boots and white stockings. Grey period wig.

Carl Linden—Dark grey period suit. Striped blue and white wing collar, shirt and cuffs. Black elastic-sided or button boots. Side burns.

The Hon. Hugh Devon—Brown frock coat. Grey check trousers. White wing collar, shirt and cuffs. Black elastic-sided boots. He is carrying gloves but is assumed to have left his hat outside. Side burns.

Scene Three

*The **Millicks**' ballroom 1875.*

Sarah—White moire period evening dress, with circular train. Gold spangled white net drape on skirt. Cameo brooch. Necklace and earrings. Period wig. At end of scene she has a short deep green period opera cloak trimmed with black. Green velvet hat trimmed with black and having a bow under the chin. White satin shoes. White silk stockings.

Mrs. Millick—Shot blue and beige taffeta period evening dress trimmed with black velvet and appliqué. Grey period wig. Diamond necklace, earrings and bracelet. Satin shoes to match. White silk stockings. Fan.

Lady Devon—Light grey bengaline period evening dress trimmed with pearls and cream lace. White period wig. Satin shoes to match. White silk stockings. Violets in hair and violet posy. Pearl necklace and ear-rings. Gold bracelet on right wrist. Fan.

Harriet—Grey satin period evening dress with pale green drapery. Auburn period wig. Satin shoes to match. White silk stockings. Fan. Jewellery to suit.

Victoria—Rose taffeta period evening dress trimmed with grey lace. Pink and red underskirt. Brown period wig. White silk stockings. Satin shoes to match. Fan. Jewellery to suit.

Honor—Blue taffeta period evening dress trimmed with pale green. Black period wig. White silk stockings. Satin shoes to match. Fan. Jewellery to suit.

Effie—Pink taffeta period evening dress trimmed with lace and rosebuds. Blonde period wig. White silk stockings. Satin shoes to match. Fan. Jewellery to suit.

Jane—Oyster satin period evening dress trimmed with black velvet. Light-brown period wig. White silk stockings. Satin shoes to match. Fan. Jewellery to suit.

Gloria—Green velvet period bodice and green chiffon skirt trimmed with pink roses and green taffeta bustle. Red period wig. White silk stockings. Satin shoes to match. Fan. Jewellery to suit.

Chaperones—About three or four of the chorus may be dressed to represent chaperones. Dresses of brown taffeta, blue satin velvet and gold satin, etc. Grey or white wigs. White stockings. Satin shoes to match. Fans. Jewellery to suit.

Chorus Ladies—In general the dresses follow the descriptions given above. Suggested colours: Blue satin trimmed tan; check silk taffeta trimmed brown velvet; pale blue taffeta trimmed beige moire ribbon; red taffeta trimmed green; pink taffeta trimmed apple green; mauve taffeta trimmed narrow flounces of mauve and white; grey, white and cerise skirt with cerise velvet bodice; deep red velvet trimmed black and white lace; terra-cotta satin trimmed gold brocade; rose and blue shot taffeta trimmed blue and grey shot taffeta and silver tassels; pale pink taffeta with pleated green edged frills; mole and blue brocade trimmed fawn net; apple-green velvet trimmed blue velvet and convolvulus.

General Note on Ladies' Costumes

The shoes do not show very much and as long as they match the costumes they need not be absolutely to period. The heels should be fairly low. In place of petticoats, frills may be sewn on the insides of the skirts. These are very necessary for the polka. Small Victorian posies can be worn in the hair in most cases. Everyone should have white button gloves coming at least half-way up the forearm.

The Hon. Hugh Devon—Period full evening dress, white closed-front collar, flat white tie, dancing-pumps with bows, white kid gloves. Side burns and moustache. Pink carnation.

Carl Linden—Period full evening dress, white winged collar, flat white tie, dancing-pumps with bows. Side burns. At end of scene he has a black evening cloak, opera hat and white silk scarf. No gloves.

Sir Arthur Fenchurch—Period full evening dress, white winged collar, flat white tie. Frilled shirt front liberally splashed with claret. Claret-stained handkerchief. Dancing-pumps with bows. White wig and side burns. White kid gloves. Gardenia.

Chorus Gentlemen And Musicians—Period full evening dress, white winged collar, flat white tie, dancing-pumps with bows. White kid gloves (except musicians). Various period side burns and moustaches.

Note—Black waistcoats were worn with full evening dress at this period. Trousers were not creased.

Footmen—Wine-coloured long coats trimmed with gold braid and gold buttons. Red plush knee-breeches. White cotton stockings. Black shoes with silver buckles. White wigs curled in front and short behind. White cotton gloves.

Mr. Vale—Full evening dress of a naval lieutenant.
Mr. Proutie—Scotch regimental evening dress.
Lord Edgar James—Rifle Brigade evening dress.
Lord Sorrel—Royal Artillery evening dress.
The Marquis of Steere
Mr. Bethel } Full period evening dress.

Note—All the above six men have white kid gloves. The two civilians wear white carnations.

ACT II

Scene One

Herr Schlick's Café in Vienna at 12 noon. 1880.

Sari—Grey period dress trimmed with baby blue satin bows at neck and back of waist. Blue edging and lining to overdrape. White frills at neck and wrists. Grey capelet trimmed with blue bows and lined blue. Black felt hat trimmed with blue bow. Black buttoned boots with grey felt tops. White gloves. Period wig dressed in a simple style.

Manon—Purple-and-white plaid period dress with large bustle trimmed with full black and white pleats at neck and wrists. White gloves. Black velvet ribbon round neck. Cameo brooch. Black period wig with fringe, bun and spit curls at sides. Orange velvet hat with a white wing. Blue outdoor coatee trimmed with black fur and lined orange. Black button boots with grey cloth tops. Black stockings. Full, elaborate, frilled white petticoat.

Gussi—Beige satin skirt trimmed with beige velvet and brown velvet coatee with imitation mink fur edgings at cuffs, neck, and round bottom, and having black braid frogs across the front. Mink muff. Beige velvet hat trimmed with mink and cock's feathers. Beige buttoned boots with cloth tops. Blonde period wig. Black stockings. White gloves.

Hansi—Plaid skirt and blue coatee trimmed with fur at cuffs and round bottom. Bows down front. Blue felt hat trimmed with wings and red ribbon tying under the chin. Red period wig. Black buttoned boots with cloth tops. Black stockings. White gloves.

Freda—Dark blue skirt striped with darker blue and trimmed with black. Light blue coat trimmed with black, dark blue and buttons. Blue felt hat trimmed with black and white bird wings and blue ribbon. Blonde period wig. Black stockings. White gloves.

Lotte—Grey skirt. Rose coatee trimmed with white fur. Rose felt hat trimmed with grey wing feathers. Brown period wig. Black stockings. Black button boots.

General Note on **Gussi**, **Hansi**, **Freda** and **Lotte**

All skirts have elaborate bustles for "The Ladies of the Town" number. All carry white handkerchiefs tucked into their left cuffs for the business in the same number. Petticoats need not be worn.

Cleaners And Charwomen—Rough dull-coloured skirts and loose blouses. Some have shawls over their heads. Old black elastic-sided or button boots. Black stockings.

Carl—Fawn trousers. Light grey waistcoat. White shirt and wing collar with large soft grey bow-tie. Grey velvet lounge coat. (He opens the scene in his shirt sleeves.) Elastic-sided black and grey boots. At end of scene he carries a grey overcoat and brown hat. Side burns.

Schlick—Brown trousers. Brown-and-white check coat and waistcoat. Very open wing collar and large soft white bow-tie. Red bandanna handkerchief hanging out of his left coat pocket. Semi-bald black wig with quiff. Side burns and large black curling moustache. Brown carpet slippers.

Captain August Lutte—Uniform consisting of light grey trousers strapped under elastic-sided boots (black). Long navy blue greatcoat piped with red. Sword (worn inside coat), sword knot and spurs—silver, upturned. Eyeglass and cord. Very long cigarette-holder. High peaked uniform hat. White kid gloves. Black military moustache and side burns.

Fritz And Other Waiters—Black trousers, stiff white shirt fronts. No collars, waistcoats or coats. Various coloured baize aprons with bibs. Old slippers or boots.

Musicians—Pepper-and-salt nondescript period suits with wing collars and odd ties. Period bowler and felt hats which may be worn during the scene.

Scene Two

Herr Schlick's *Café in Vienna—2 a.m. 1880.*

Sari—White satin period evening dress trimmed with lace. White satin shoes and white silk stockings. Same wig as last scene.

Manon—Red spangled period ballet dress with short skirt above knees, trimmed with bluish green spangled insets. Pale blue, bright green and red gauze petticoats. Red gauze frilled drawers. Red gauze bow at neck. Long black gloves. Black silk opera hose. Black shoes with high blue tops laced with black and having black tassels. Period wig, more elaborately dressed than last scene.

Gussi—White lace period dress with primrose silk bodice and overdrape. White lace and primrose hat with beige pom-pom. White satin shoes and white stockings. White long gloves. Same wig as last scene.

Hansi—Pink and white satin period evening dress. Pink satin shoes. White stockings. Long white gloves. Same wig as last scene.

Freda—Crimson satin period dress trimmed with lace. Lace hat trimmed with crimson satin. Crimson satin shoes. White stockings. Long white gloves. Same wig as last scene.

Lotte—Black, white and green silk period dress lined with green. Fawn felt hat with green feathers. Black satin shoes. White stockings. Black gloves. Same wig as last scene.

Lady Patrons—Various period dresses as follows: Green plaid street dress, white waistcoat, blue felt hat and green band; green brocade evening dress with rose-pink front, green shoes, elaborate jewellery and black wig; brown and brocade evening dress trimmed with large buckles; blue velvet trimmed with rose, blue and white and cream net and pink ribbon hat; brown and orange cloth with brown hat trimmed with nasturtiums; green and white foulard evening dress; mauve satin dress with mauve ribbon hat; primrose silk trimmed with white lace and white lace hat trimmed with a feather; grey street dress with black spots, trimmed with black, black hat trimmed with black velvet; black and white check street dress, white felt hat trimmed with black and cat's-eye necklace; white dress with large green spots trimmed with cream lace, green velvet hat.

Many wigs, shoes, stockings and gloves can be doubled from Act I, Scene Three. Flowers and bows can be worn in the hair.

Carl—Same trousers, shirt, collar and boots as last scene. Evening tail coat, white waistcoat, white silk soft bow-tie. Side burns.

Schlick—Full period evening dress with very open wing collar and large black tie. Same hair as last scene. Black evening shoes. Large carnation. Large gold watch-chain.

Captain August Lutte—Same trousers and boots, spurs, cigarette-holder, eyeglass and cord and white gloves as last scene. Black military moustache and side burns. Tunic of black cloth and silver braid. He does not wear a hat or sword in this scene.

Lieutenant Tranisch—Same uniform as Captain Lutte.

Musicians—Same as Act I, Scene Three, except that they have black ties.

Civilian Patrons—Various pepper-and-salt period suits, elastic-sided boots, whiskers, bowler and felt hats.

Waiters—Same as Musicians.

Officers—Five of them have blue tunics and grey trousers strapped under elastic-sided black boots with silver spurs. Two have black tunics and grey trousers and one has brown tunic and black trousers. High peaked uniform hats. Side burns and moustaches.

Note—If thought desirable, Tranisch can have one of these uniforms.

Prater Girls—Three are dressed as peasant girls, having short ballet skirts, white frilled petticoats and drawers. One dress has purple and white material, one has blue and white and one has rose and white, the colour being the base and the spots white. White frilled aprons. Black buttoned boots with high beige cloth tops. Low heels. White stockings. Handkerchiefs over hair to match dress.

The other three girls are dressed as boys in long tight brown plaid trousers. Red-and-white striped stockings. Black waistcoats. Green aprons with bibs. Green alpine hats with long green feathers. Ballet shirts and black ballet shoes.

Note—The three girls have large property laundry baskets fastened on their shoulders.

ACT III

Scene One

Lord Shayne's *house. 1895.*

Sari—White satin period evening dress with large puffed sleeves and stiff black lace epaulettes. Period wig. Aigrette and diamanté brooch in hair. Ear-rings. White flowers in diamond brooch in corsage. Fan of long black tipped white plumes. White satin shoes. White silk stockings. Long white kid gloves above elbows.

Mrs. Devon— (Note. —This is not the same person as Lady Devon in Act I, Scene Three.) Grey brocade period evening dress trimmed with cream lace and jet. Brown period wig trimmed with jet ornaments and aigrette. Grey satin shoes. White stockings. Long white gloves and feather fan. Jewellery to suit. Fan.

Harriet—Green velvet period evening dress trimmed with black feathers. White satin petticoat. Auburn period wig with black feathers. Green satin shoes. White stockings. Long white gloves. Jewellery to suit. Fan.

Gloria—Black satin period evening dress trimmed with peach. Red wig with jet comb. Black satin shoes. Black stockings. Long black gloves. Jewellery to suit. Fan.

Jane—Gold and grey period evening dress trimmed with lace. Light brown period wig with fringe. Gold brocade shoes. White stockings. Long white gloves. Jewellery to suit. Fan.

Effie—Gold brocade period evening dress with lace panels in skirt. White wig with diamanté bandeau. Gold brocade shoes. White stockings. Long white gloves. Jewellery to suit. Fan.

Honor—White silk period evening dress with painted iris flowers and amethyst velvet sleeves, trimmed with jet. Black period wig with diamanté bandeau. White satin shoes. White stockings. Long white gloves. Jewellery to suit. Fan.

Victoria—Mauve satin period evening dress trimmed with lace. Brown wig with diamanté bow. Mauve satin period shoes. White stockings. Jewellery to suit. Fan.

Chorus Ladies—In general the dresses follow the descriptions given above. Suggested ensembles: Flowers on white satin ground, trimmed white chiffon and black baby velvet; plain yellow satin princess robe trimmed powder blue silk; strawberry bengaline, trimmed black net, blue velvet and flowers; grey and blue shot brocade, trimmed pink velvet and black net; gold satin princess robe, trimmed brown velvet and embroidered sleeves; very pale pink silk, trimmed lace and mauve ribbons; grey brocade, trimmed blue and rosebuds; striped pink-and-white brocade skirt, grey velvet bodice trimmed with small pearls; grey silk, trimmed with black velvet and white lace; mauve satin with a lace front panel; grey brocade trimmed pink velvet with lines of fine jet beads; pale green satin with pink satin sleeves and brocade panels; pink satin with long sleeves, trimmed with brocade; green brocade trimmed with claret velvet.

General Note on Ladies' Costumes

The same shoes that were worn in Act I, Scene Three, can be worn provided they are a near match to the costumes. Fans are mostly lace, though some feather and Japanese fans can be used. Other accessories as above.

Marquis of Shayne—Period full evening dress, white waistcoat. White period wig and moustache. White gloves. Black dancing-pumps. Red rosette of Légion d'Honneur in left lapel.

Hugh Devon, **Accompanist**, **Chorus Gentlemen**—Period full evening dress, white waistcoats. Period wigs. Various moustaches. Some wear old-fashioned eyeglasses with cords. Collars are generally closed-front type. Black dancing-pumps. White kid gloves. Hugh has grey wig.

"Green Carnation" Boys—As for other men but more effeminate in details and each one having a large green carnation in his buttonhole.

Butler—As other men, but with black tie and waistcoat.

Scene Two

Lady Shayne's *house. Present Day.*

All exactly as ACT I, Scene One.

PROPERTY PLOT

Note—The essential properties are marked with asterisks. The other properties may be varied at the convenience of the producer. They are included in this list as a guide to what should be used.

ACT I

Scene One

Lady Shayne's *house in Grosvenor Square. Present day.*

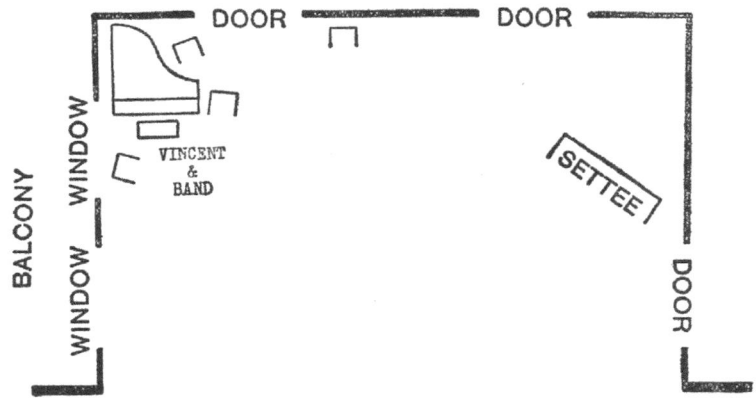

*1 baby grand piano up right.
*1 megaphone on piano.
*3 gilt cane chairs and 1 piano-stool up right.
1 gilt cane chair between windows right.
1 gilt cane chair down stage right.
*1 jazz drum up right.
*2 drums on top of jazz drum.
*1 tap-box up right.
*1 small drum and stand up right.
*1 pair of foot cymbals up right.
1 Empire armchair up centre by wall.
1 Empire table with bowl of flowers, cigarette-box and ash-tray up centre by wall—on left of armchair.
1 pedestal and bowl in niche in wall up centre.
1 pedestal and bowl in niche in wall up left.
1 semicircular table with vase of flowers up left.
1 four-fold screen up left.

*1 Empire settee and squab in front of screen up left.
*1 Empire table, cigarette-box, match-stand and bowl of flowers down left.
2 pairs of green and white curtains and pelmets to windows right.
2 pairs of white net curtains to same.
*1 walking stick for Lady Shayne—personal property.

Outside double doors up left.

1 extending-leaf mahogany table having on it:
    1 long d'oyley.
    6 small d'oyleys.
    6 green plates (fruit).
    6 sets knives, forks and spoons.
    6 champagne glasses.
    12 table napkins.
    Note.—Six of these should be used and substituted for the clean ones during the action of the scene.
    6 green coffee-cups, saucers and spoons.
6 gilt cane chairs.
3 pairs of green canvas curtains on backing.

Outside double doors up right.

1 small table.
1 oil painting in gilt frame.
    Note.—The reversible panels, in this scene, are turned so that they show their painted sides or, in some cases, those sides which match the walls.

See picture of scene.

Scene Two

*The **Millicks'** house in Belgrave Square. 1875.*

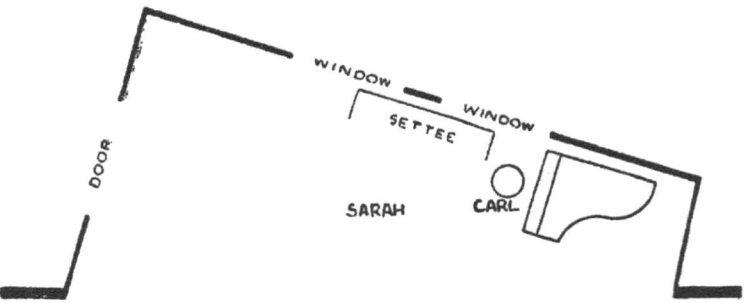

1 stage-cloth painted as carpet.
2 pairs of pink curtains, pelmets and tie-backs to windows up centre.
2 pairs of white lace curtains and tie-backs to windows up centre.
2 green Venetian blinds to windows up centre.
*1 full-size period grand piano—keys to right, slightly oblique.
*1 circular red plush piano stool on right of piano.
On piano. —1 circular patchwork piano cover.
    1 alabaster horn vase of flowers, forget-me-nots and roses.
    1 lot music on rest.
*1 plush single-ended sofa up centre.
1 pedestal with plush cover in corner up right.
1 blue glass oil lamp and white globe on pedestal.
1 maple-framed picture of boy and dog on wall up left.
1 gilt-framed picture of boy on wall up right.
1 black-framed picture of flowers on wall down right.

Scene Three

The Ballroom of the **Millicks'** *house in Bilgrave Square. 1875.*

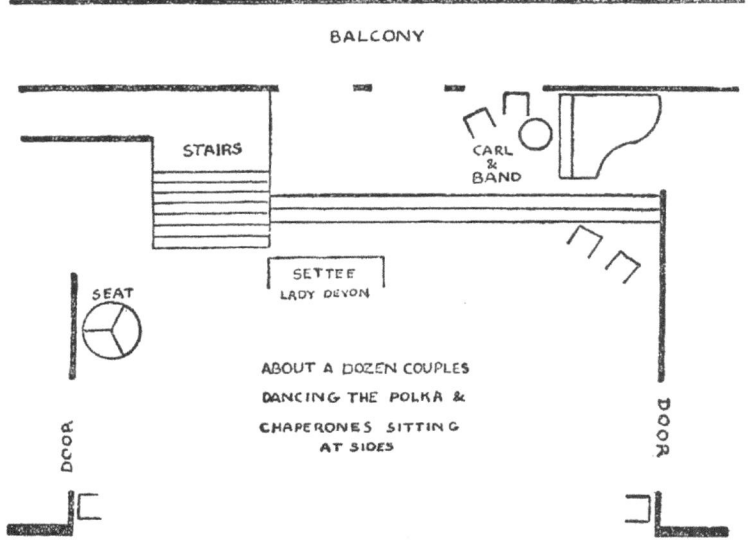

1 large red plush settee on rostrum at top of stairs up right.
1 large red plush circular seat at right foot of stairs.
*2 striped silk single chairs down right.
*1 two-wing red plush couch at left foot of stairs.
*2 striped silk single chairs up stage centre below steps.
*2 red plush single chairs up stage left below steps.
1 gilt jardinière with ferns, palms and flowers behind plush chairs up stage left.
*1 striped silk single chair down left.
1 gilt console table with vase of flowers down left.
3 pairs of yellow curtains and pelmets on the three windows up stage.
1 set of yellow curtains and tie-backs for stair arches.
2 yellow curtains and tie-backs for entrances down right and left.
1 gilt compo mirror on wall over settee on rostrum up right.
1 mahogany framed mirror on wall down left.
2 papier-mâché bowls with palm leaves on stair pedestals right and left.
On Rostrum up centre—*4 gilt cane chairs on left.
   *3 gilt music stands and music on each on left.
   *1 grand piano and music (doubled from Act I, Scene Two) on left.
   *1 circular red plush piano-stool (doubled from Act I, Scene Two).
   2 striped silk armchairs by columns.
   *1 violin and bow on piano.
*4 long poles for turning out gas, for Footmen, off left.
*1 large handkerchief for use as blindfold for Effie—personal property (Wardrobe).
*1 claret-stained handkerchief for Sir Arthur Fenchurch—personal property (Wardrobe).
*Opera hat, scarf (white silk) and black evening coat for Carl (Wardrobe).
*Bonnet and cape for Sarah (Wardrobe).
2 lighted candles—one off down right and one off down left.
   Note.—Effie's handkerchief should be obtained from Sarah at a convenient moment during the scene and retained by Effie for the next performance. The clothes for Carl and Sarah should be obtained from them by the property master at the end of the scene, and he is responsible that they are ready off stage each night, at the entrance up right.
   Quantity of dance programmes.

ACT II

Scene One

Herr Schlick's *Café in Vienna—12 o'clock noon. 1880.*

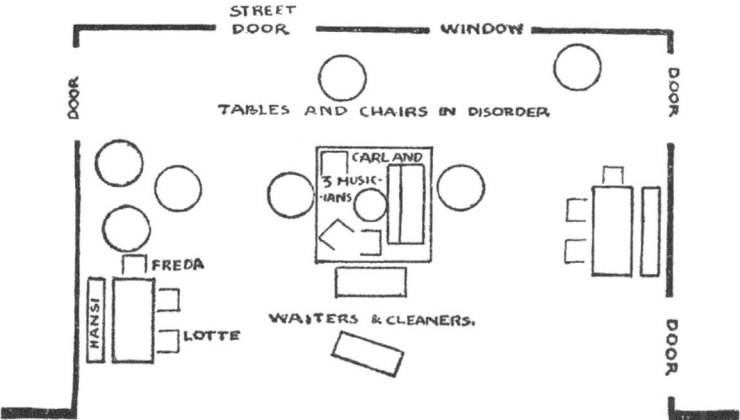

*3 circular tables on rostrum up right.
*11 Bentwood chairs on rostrum up right.
*1 red plush settee down right.
*1 large table in front of settee down right.
On Table. —1 tray, 3 coffee glasses and spoons, 3 wine-glasses, 1 ash-tray, 1 sugar-bowl, 2 plates of brioche.
*1 old-fashioned upright piano, 3 music stands and music, 3 chairs, 1 stool, and 1 violin and bow, all on bandstand centre.
2 violin bags, 1 cup, saucer and spoon and duster on balustrade round bandstand.
*1 small table below bandstand centre.
*2 Bentwood chairs below bandstand centre.
*3 sweeping-brooms on right side of bandstand.
*2 water buckets and swabs on right side of bandstand.
*1 water bucket and swab down stage centre.
*1 dustpan and brush by right centre column.
1 small circular table on right side of bandstand.
1 Bentwood chair upside down on table right side of bandstand.
1 red check tablecloth on table on right side of bandstand.
2 circular tables on left side of bandstand.
2 Bentwood chairs on above tables.
1 large tiled stove with pail of coke and shovel up left by wall.
1 large property swan on top of stove.

3 Bentwood chairs by stove.
*1 large table down left.
*1 plush settee down left by wall.
*3 Bentwood chairs on above table.
*9 dusters, 1 plate and swab and 1 red check tablecloth on above table.
*4 circular tables on rostrum at back.
*17 Bentwood chairs on rostrum at back.
1 small table right down stage centre.
3 Bentwood chairs on above table.
5 café sign tablets on panels of walls.
*2 brackets with 3 fencing-foils in each on panels down right and left.
1 pair of red and yellow plush curtains and pelmet on opening down left.
1 pair of red casement curtains on street door up right centre.
1 pair of red casement curtains on window up left centre.
*2 coins for Freda—personal property.
*1 cigarette-holder and 1 cigarette per performance for Captain Lutte—personal property.
6 cigars per performance for Bandsmen, Waiters, etc.
*1 tray with coffee and straws for Waiter off up right
*1 bill for Waiter off up right.
*1 tray with 2 coffee-glasses, 2 spoons, 1 plate of brioche and sugar-bowl for Waiter off up right.
*4 handkerchiefs for Gussi, Hansi, Lotte and Freda.

Scene Two

Herr Schlick's *Café in Vienna*—2 a.m. 1880.

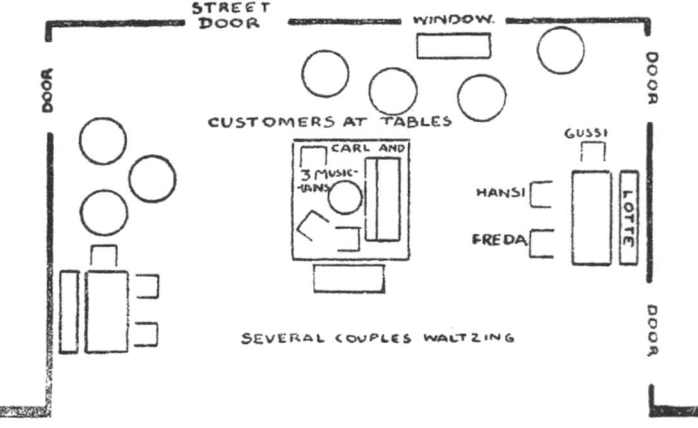

Note. —This is the same as Act II, Scene One, but now the place has been re-arranged for the customers. The tables, with the exception of the one right down stage centre, are in the same general positions. The one down centre has been taken to the back. All tables have red check tablecloths. The chairs are arranged round them. Scattered about on the tables are several news-papers, cups and saucers, glasses, ash-trays and bottles.

Off stage up right are three trays with a quantity of wine bottles, tokay glasses (small red tumblers), beer mugs, napkins, bill pads for Waiters and 3 laundry baskets for 3 Prater Girls.

Among the patrons are distributed various cigarettes, cigars, walking-sticks, umbrellas, spectacles, watches and chains and coins.

Lutte and Tranisch have cigarettes in holders.

Schlick has a cigar.

In order to prevent striking of matches the Waiters can have tapers for which they are responsible.

ACT III

Scene One

Lord Shayne's *house in Grosvenor Square. 1895.*

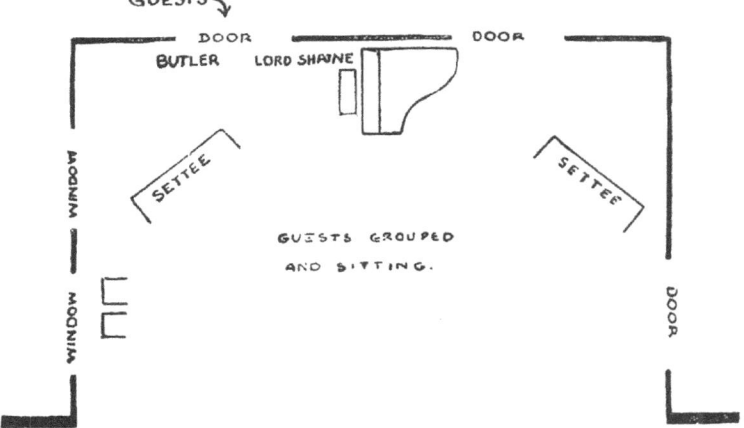

Note. —This is the same set as Act I, Scene One. The reversible panels in the walls are turned so that the flowered sides face the audience.

1 Aubusson carpet centre.

2 pairs of rose-pink tapestry curtains and pelmets for windows right.
2 single white net curtains for same.
*1 tub rail tapestry chair down right.
*1 Empire armchair (doubled from ACT I, Scene One) down right.
1 semicircular table between windows right.
1 alabaster figure on above table.
1 oak easel and Marcus Stone picture in corner up right.
*1 gilt armchair in front of easel up right.
*1 gilt tapestry settee in front of above chair.
1 rose-pink tapestry and glass screen on left of doors up right.
1 iron palmstand and palm on right of above screen.
*1 grand piano (same as ACT I, Scene Two), music on it, and piano stool.
1 fringed tapestry piano cover on piano.
1 bowl of lilac flowers on piano.
1 Empire table up left in corner (same as ACT I, Scene One).
1 vase of lilac and pink carnations on above table.
1 photo frame on above table.
2 gilt tapestry armchairs down stage of above table.
*1 Empire settee and squab (same as ACT I, Scene One) in front of above chairs.
1 Empire table below door l. (same as ACT I, Scene One).
1 cream-and-gold runner on above table.
1 photo frame on above table.
1 flower-vase.
2 pedestals and vases in niches in upstage wall (as Act I, Scene One).
1 plush framed plaque on panel up right.
1 gilt framed oil painting below plaque on same panel.
2 oval gilt photo-frames on panel left of door up right.
1 plush and gilt photo-frame on panel above upper window right.
1 gilt framed oil painting on panel up left.
2 plush framed photos on panel upstage of door down left.
1 plush framed circular plaque of flowers above door down left.
1 gilt mirror with candle sconces on panel downstage of door down left.
1 bookcase against backing outside doors up right.
1 tray of visiting-cards on above table.
1 photo in plush frame on above table.

1 vase of ferns on above table.
1 gilt framed oil landscape on backing over above table.
3 pairs brown curtains on backing outside doors up left.
7 gilt cane seat single chairs against above backing.
1 gilt tall jardinière stand and azaleas against above backing.

Scene Two

Exactly the same as ACT I, Scene One.

As the opening of this scene is supposed to be continuous with the closing of Act I, Scene One, everything possible should be done to change the details of the last scene, ACT III, Scene One, to what they were in ACT I, Scene One. The panels in the walls are reversed. The piano is changed. The carpet is taken up. The pictures and photo frames are removed and furniture altered. The double doors up left can be left shut so that it is not necessary to change the properties outside these. The change should be done at the utmost speed.

ELECTRICAL FITTINGS

ACT I

Scene One

4 mirror brackets—2-light, with shades on walls.
2 Georgian candelabra—3-light, with shades on table outside door up left.

Scene Two

1 oil lamp with shade on pedestal up right unlit.

Scene Three

1 cut-glass chandelier with gas globes hanging centre.
2 3-light gas brackets.
2 9-light stair fittings with fancy shades on each side of stairs.

ACT II

Scene One

6 gas arches
5 double gas brackets
12 single gas brackets
3 gas chandeliers
} On scene, all with buckram globes.

1 square red lamp outside street door up right centre.

All above unlit.

Scene Two

All as above for ACT II, Scene One, but alight.

ACT III

Scene One

1 floor standard lamp with flounced period shade up stage of piano.
2 oil lamps with flounced period shades on tables right and left.

All fittings to be alight unless otherwise stated.

Note.—In addition to the various lead and plug boards required for the above fittings, 2 lengths of 1½-inch barrel will be wanted for the stair fittings and a chain, steel wire and ceiling block for the centre fitting in ACT I, Scene Three. Most of the above fittings are required for "atmosphere" only and could be dispensed with on the score of economy.

LIGHTING REQUIREMENTS

The footlights and battens should be provided with one circuit each of pink, amber, blue and white. If only three circuits are available the pink and ambers may be mixed. Any hanging floods available should be used to re-inforce the batten lighting.

About 8 1,000-watt spots, focused on the important points of the acting area, are wanted. They should all have pale amber and frost mediums except one, which is blue. This blue spot is focused down right centre to pick up the group at the end of ACT I, Scene Three, when Carl and Sarah say goodbye to the girls.

It is an advantage to have two or three front-of-the-house arcs with pale amber and frost mediums.

If it is not possible to have so many fixed spots, a smaller number reinforced by perch spots would answer, but it should be remembered that this play is more naturalistic than most musical comedies and that perch spots should be used with care.

In general the lighting should be kept as bright as is consistent with bringing out the delicate colouring of the dresses.

The plot which follows (and which is printed in the text opposite the respective cues) is a suggested plan only and must be amplified at the actual lighting rehearsal.

GENERAL LIGHTING PLOT

ACT I

Scene One

Lady Shayne's *house.*

To Open.—Pink, white and amber in floats and battens. Lengths, floods and spots as required. Fittings alight.

At cue, repeat of "Tho' Fate may Cheat You," gradually check out everything, the last to go being a front-of-house white spot on Lady Shayne, which dies out on last word of song.

At cue, curtain down, working light on. Keep on until change is complete, then black out.

Scene Two

The **Millicks'** *house.*

To Open. —As curtain rises, fade in slowly floats white and amber to ¾; lengths, floods and spots as required; fittings out.

At cue, curtain down, front-of-house arc and floats out.

Scene Three

The **Millicks'** *ballroom.*

To Open. —Full up everything. Fittings alight.

At cue, as Blind Man's Buff starts, fade in floats blue to full.

At cue, as Footmen turn out the gas, black out everything except blue floats and backcloth lighting.

At cue, as people group at right centre, bring up special blue spot and one front-of-house white arc.

At cue, curtain down, front-of-house arc and floats out.

ACT II

Scene One

Herr Schlick's *Café—Morning.*

To Open. —Floats (white) at ¼. Floats (blue) at full. Battens (blue) at ½. Lengths, spots and floods as required. Fittings out.

At cue, end of opening chorus, bring white floats up to ¾.

At cue, "That the *World* will be Jealous," fade out everything so that there is a complete black out by the time the last word of the number is sung.

At cue, curtain down, working light.

Scene Two

Herr Schlick's *Café—Night.*

To Open. —Full up everything. Fittings alight.
At cue, curtain down, front-of-house arcs and floats out.

ACT III

Scene One

Lord Shayne's *house.*

To Open. —Full up everything.

At cue, "World has gone *awry*," fade out everything, the last to go being a white front-of-house spot on Sari which dies out on "Goodbye."

At cue, curtain down, working light.

Scene Two

Same as Act I, Scene One.

At cue, as curtain rises, bring up everything slowly to ACT I, Scene One, light.

At cue, curtain down, front-of-house arcs out.

For Calls. —Everything full up.

Note. —Front-of-house arcs and floats come up slowly to mark on plot each time the curtain rises.

House lights are put up only between the Acts.

ABOUT THE AUTHOR

Noël Peirce Coward was born in 1899 and made his professional stage debut as Prince Mussel in *The Goldfish* at the age of twelve, leading to many child actor appearances over the next few years. His breakthrough in playwriting was the controversial *The Vortex* (1924) which featured themes of drugs and adultery and made his name as both actor and playwright in the West End and on Broadway. During the frenzied 1920s and the more sedate 1930s, Coward wrote a string of successful plays, musicals and intimate revues including *Fallen Angels* (1925), *Hay Fever* (1925), *Easy Virtue* (1926), *This Year of Grace* (1928), and *Bitter Sweet* (1929). His professional partnership with childhood friend Gertrude Lawrence, started with *Private Lives* (1931), and continued with *Tonight at 8.30* (1936).

During World War II, he remained a successful playwright, screenwriter and director, as well as entertaining the troops and even acting as an unofficial spy for the Foreign Office. His plays during these years included *Blithe Spirit*, which ran for 1,997 performances, outlasting the War (a West End record until *The Mousetrap* overtook it), *This Happy Breed* and *Present Laughter* (both 1943). His two wartime screenplays, *In Which We Serve*, which he co-directed with the young David Lean, and *Brief Encounter* quickly became classics of British cinema.

However, the post-war years were more difficult. Austerity Britain – the London critics determined – was out of tune with the brittle Coward wit. In response, Coward re-invented himself as a cabaret and TV star, particularly in America, and in 1955 he played a sell-out season in Las Vegas featuring many of his most famous songs, including *Mad About the Boy*, *I'll See You Again* and *Mad Dogs and Englishmen*. In the mid-1950s he settled in Jamaica and Switzerland, and enjoyed a renaissance in the early 1960s becoming the first living playwright to be performed by the National Theatre, when he directed *Hay Fever* there. Late in his career he was lauded for his roles in a number of films including *Our Man In Havana* (1959) and his role as the iconic Mr Bridger alongside Michael Caine in *The Italian Job* (1968).

Writer, actor, director, film producer, painter, songwriter, cabaret artist as well as an author of a novel, verse, essays and autobiographies, he was called by close friends 'The Master'. His final West End appearance was *Song at Twilight* in 1966, which he wrote and starred in. He was knighted in 1970 and died peacefully in 1973 in his beloved Jamaica.

For further information on Noël Coward's life and work, visit www.noelcoward.com and to join the Noël Coward Society, visit www.noelcoward.net.

**Other plays by NOËL COWARD
published and licensed by Concord Theatricals**

Blithe Spirit

Come into the Garden Maud

Fumed Oak

Hay Fever

I'll Leave It to You

Present Laughter

Private Lives

Relative Values

Still Life

This Happy Breed

This Was A Man

Waiting in the Wings

FIND PERFECT PLAYS TO PERFORM AT
www.concordtheatricals.co.uk

www.ingramcontent.com/pod-product-compliance
Ingram Content Group UK Ltd.
Pitfield, Milton Keynes, MK11 3LW, UK
UKHW021843210426
5322IPUK00022B/431